WISE IN
THE ROAD...

WISE IN THE ROAD...

A pod of vignettes of memories, moments, mischief, and maturity—reminiscences, reminders, remembrances and recalls along the "Y's" in the life of Edwards Ritchie Hopple.

EDWARDS R. HOPPLE

Library of Congress Control Number:		2009900406
ISBN:	Hardcover	978-1-4415-0358-9
	Softcover	978-1-4415-0357-2

To order additional copies of this book, contact:
Xlibris Corporation
1-888-795-4274
www.Xlibris.com
Orders@Xlibris.com
35249

THOSE WHO MADE A DIFFERENCE AT THE VARIOUS "Y's" IN MY ROAD OF LIFE, I THANK EACH ONE FOR HIS OR HER CONTRIBUTION TO MY DIRECTIONS:

MY PARENTS—They guided me. They taught me. They helped me. Most of all, they loved me. I couldn't have had better, nicer, more informative and fun-loving parents than Mom and Dad. Whatever I am, they made me.

ROBERT HECHT—I was 18 when he gambled on me to drive him all over the country. The 7-week trip opened my eyes to the USA . . . and his counsel I honor to this day. He matured me.

BOB VANCE—A lifelong friend from Amherst College. We were in business together, and he set the stages for my advancing in entrepreneurship and broadcasting. I'll always be grateful.

WONDERFUL WIFE CATHIE—A beautiful girl! A perfect lady! A wonderful wife! She was willing to take risks. Moving West took guts and she had 'em. We had 46+ years of being happily married and I would not trade a day! She left too early and deserved better . . . but the man upstairs knows when. I'll join her soon!

DON DOBSON—A neat guy I met in the Army and he is the one who put us together on the Tahoe Biltmore venture. That got us West . . . and we never left!

JACKIE GAUGHAN—When we returned to NYC after the Biltmore scenario, he got me the job of Ad guy at the Flamingo Hotel in Las Vegas. He was wonderful to us while we were in Vegas and helped us around town. It was there we adopted two of our three daughters.

GORDON SHERWOOD—He and wife Jan befriended us in Vegas, and I finally went to work at KENO Radio which he managed. Together we built it up, sold it and bought KMAP in Bakersfield, California. He taught me commercial broadcasting. When he left for his hometown Seattle, I was left to run KMAP, Inc's Radio KWAC. The next 40 years are history! We still met and talked about the old days . . . and laughed a lot. I thank him for being a good friend and mentor.

ALL OF BAKERSFIELD—When I came to Bakersfield it was supposed to be for a short time, and then on to another market. We never left . . . and I am SO glad. The people, the customers, the friends, and the competitors were all terrific. It has been a great life, and I've tried to give back to the community and friends who made it all possible. Everyone should be so lucky!!!

WISE IN THE ROAD...

A pod of vignettes of memories, moments, mischief, and maturity—reminiscences, reminders, remembrances and recalls along the "Y's" in the life of Edwards Ritchie Hopple.

Born January 6, 1930 in Cincinnati, Ohio
"Cashed In" at Age_____
on_____, 20____ in_____

When the time comes, friends may fill in the blanks to close the ERH era.
ONE GREAT RIDE!

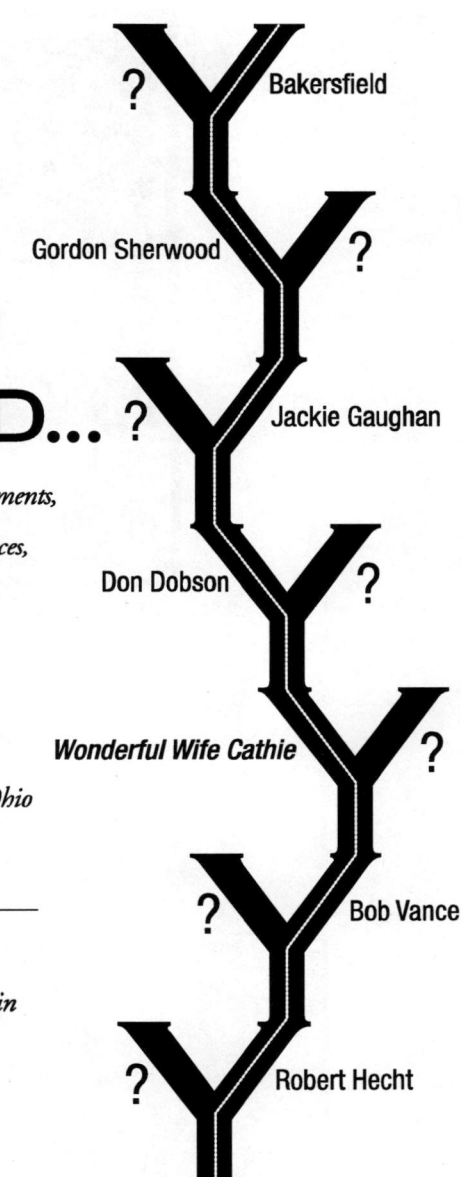

? Bakersfield

Gordon Sherwood ?

? Jackie Gaughan

Don Dobson ?

Wonderful Wife Cathie ?

? Bob Vance

? Robert Hecht

Parents ?

January 6, 1930

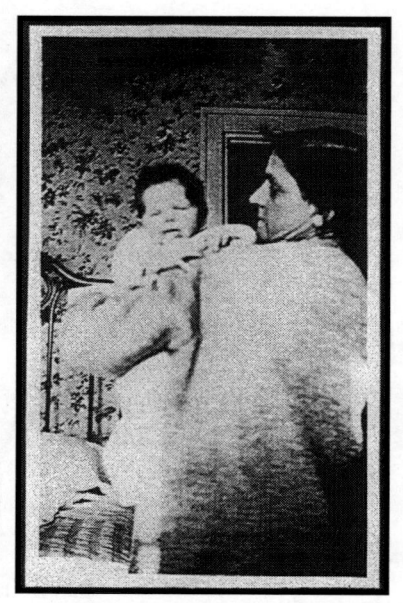

THE STARTING GATE

IN THE HOME STRETCH

PREFACE

I dedicate this book to the individuals and places at the "Y's" in the road. I'm not able to pile it all together in a neat and comprehensive pile, but I tried to get some chronology in it to give anyone who cares to read it an insight into my history.

The major figure in 46+ years of my life was wife Cathie. She put up with me, and that took some doing. I loved every minute!!!

The book is divided into three sections. The first contains paragraphs of things I remember and things that were important. The second so-called section contains details of certain events, probably found in the first section. You will know when the first section ends that you are starting on the second. Same idea for the third where there are a bunch of certificates, letters, etc. that I thought were worth keeping.

All in all it empties my brain, some bulletin boards, some files and file drawers. That probably makes it all worthwhile. I hope you enjoy something in it . . . as I always say . . . Cheers! Don't draw to fill! See you in the funny papers! Write if you get work!

EH—Summer 2009

PRELUDE

Which comes first . . . Preface or Prelude? I don't know and really don't care. Shuffle as you wish. In doing this I find that I have lost all sense of spelling, grammar, syntax, and symmetry. It is what it is! I think that people who know me would say that he wrote it the way he talks. I guess that's OK. In an effort to help the perfectionists among readers (if there are any . . . either readers or perfectionists), I am including a GRAMMAR & PUNCTUATION LOCKER.

It is located on this page. Readers that feel they must change words or punctuation marks are welcome to take from the locker, or return to the locker. If the locker overflows, throw items away. If the locker is short, find one on any computer keyboard. OK?

LOCKER

. . . . ? ? ? ? ? ? ? ? ? ? , , , , , , , , , , , " " " " " " " "

" " " !!!!!!!!!! ((((((((()))))))))) ----------

& & & & & & & & & & : : : : : : : : : : * * * * * * * * * *

; ; ; ; ; ; ; ; ; ; ; ; ; # # # # # # # # # # ^ ^ ^ ^ ^ ^ ^ ^

= = = = = = = = = = = + + + + + + + + + + / / / / / / / / / / @
@ @ @ @ @ @ @ @ @ $ $ $ $ $ $ $ $ $ $ _ _ _ _ _ _ _

' ' ' ' ' ' ' ' ' ' ~ ~ ~ ~ ~ ~ ~ ~ ~ ~ .

I guess Dot's Dot.

P.S. If something is *underlined* in the text, there is probably some quasi-lengthy explanation somewhere in the book.

Chapter 1 . . . THE KICKOFF

The Beginning . . . I was born on January 6, 1930 at Children's Hospital in Cincinnati, Ohio very late in the evening. My parents named me Edwards Ritchie (for my maternal grandfather) Hopple. The "Edwards" I am told originally came from Jonathan Edwards of "Sinners In The Hands of the Angry Gods" fame.

Early recollections and/or stuff I've been told about same . . . My mother did not work . . . common then . . . and she took care of me. Hattie was a (very) part-time maid and took care of me in the beginning. Mom told me I was a good baby . . . but she exaggerated a lot. When I was 3 or 4 Dell took care of me and helped my mother.

Other stuff about my early days . . . We lived in an apartment on Beech Avenue in Wyoming. We moved down the street to a house on Beech Avenue, about two blocks from the school. Incidentally, Ann Marie Lockman lived across the street and we both went K-12 in the same school building. I had a dog named Lady . . . She was blind, but I loved her. She got run over about two days after we moved to 40 Linden Drive where I grew up. My enjoyment on Sundays was to listen to Uncle Don on the radio reading the funny papers. He got fired when he thought the microphone was off and said something like "that should hold the little bastards." I loved my white coat and purple tie . . . Probably wore them to bed.

Because I was born in early January, they didn't know whether to push me ahead or stay behind starting to school. Mom took me to the school and Mr. Z.M. Walters (Superintendent) gave me some kind of a test. I must have failed because I went to kindergarten when I was five and a half. They say they asked me what was wrong with a picture of a water pitcher (it evidently had the spout and the handle on the same side.) I didn't notice that, but did say it was OK unless it leaked. I had an Irish Mail (see page 23) which I rode around on . . . It had a trailer and a license plate saying: "Repeal the 18th Amendment" . . . i.e. Prohibition.

Move to 40 Linden Drive in Wyoming . . . Before I went to 1st grade, my parents built a house at 40 Linden Drive. It was a modest house but very neat. I had built-in bunk beds. Sister Sally and I each had our own room. Mom had a sewing room. They also had a dressing room. There was a maid's room in the back with stairs to the garage. It had an outside screened sleeping porch where my sister and I used to sleep until it got too damn cold. It had all the 1st floor stuff, i.e. living room, dining room, breakfast room, kitchen, pantry etc. There was also a screened porch below the sleeping porch.

In the basement there was a finished room with a fireplace, Ping Pong table, etc. with a door out to the closed patio (below the screen and sleeping porch.) At the bottom of the stairs we had a big Hall safe with a marble top. The nickel slot machine was on top. The unfinished portion of the basement had the furnace, laundry equipment, bathroom, coal bin (it was my job to fill the stoker which pushed the coal into the furnace) . . . I also was in charge of changing the filters in the back of the furnace. These were cotton with a smooth back which Dad brought home from the Stearns & Foster mattress company where he worked all his life. They were big sheets, but I think they were made for jewelry box cotton. Incidentally, Mom used one to put around the bottom of a Christmas tree and sprinkled it with glitter. It was the beginning of the Christmas cotton you buy today.

The side yard was down a three-foot wall. It had a creek, a stone bridge across it, and a rock pool that we didn't do much with. Across the creek was a good sized grass area where we could toss a baseball. There was a street light outside which we painted black on our house side. All in all we had a good time.

Schoolmates and life long friends Bill Fischer, Bob & John Kramig, Bob Taylor, Don Baxter etc. lived close by and we usually walked the 3 blocks to school together.

Sister Sally . . . I had one sister. Her name was Sarah Hall Hopple, but she was known as Sally. She was 3 years younger than I, and we got along well. She was slightly happy go lucky . . . good looking . . . and the family had fun. She later had the "Hopple" camp at Underwood and we enjoyed each other's summers. She had been known to toss a few, but everyone loved her . . . she was the one who gathered the gang and promoted picnics (nic-a-pics) and other events. Mom did the same thing when we were young. Sal died from cancer at 65. She must have had Mom's genes, because Mom died at 52. I guess I have Dad's genes, 'cause he died at 102+ and I'm 79 and thriving pretty well. My best recollection of Sal's attitude was when we had brussels sprouts for dinner, and she wouldn't even try one. Dinner was at 6 pm sharp! Mom and Dad agreed that we would stay at the table until she tried one. We had to be excused to leave the table, so we sat and begged but she didn't budge. Around 9 pm I think they gave in, which was OK with me. I'm sure she got punished but I'm not sure how.

Some Relatives . . . Mom had an older brother, Uncle Herb Ritchie married to Aunt Helen. They had two kids, David and Susan. Mom also had an older sister, Clem Taylor (Memaw), married to Uncle Clark Taylor. They had two kids, Brice and Mary Clarkson. Brice died from something at age 17. They all lived in the small village of Wyoming where we lived so we saw some of the gang all the time. At Christmas and Thanksgiving the three families would go for breakfast (or dinner) at each other's house. Each family was on two years then off one. Memaw got her name when her son Brice couldn't say "mommy." That made Uncle Clark "Pepaw" . . . and that's what we called him.

Dad had an older sister, Aunt Ann Anderson, who was married to Uncle Bob Anderson. They had three kids, Bob (Boze), Bill, and Sis. (All three were very attentive to my Dad when he was at Dupree Terrace. I was in California, New York, or Mexico and went to see him every month for five years, but they made many visits in a month and it gave me peace that someone cared and was watching him.) All three were very good in sports at Wyoming High. Bill became a lawyer, and was Dad's lawyer with power of attorney etc. Boze worked for some time at Stearns & Foster. I remember Dad saying Boze won a Mercedes in a raffle. Sis moved to Montana and now spends her winters in Green Valley, Arizona. We would go to their house for Sunday evening snacks (Sunday main meals were at noon then). Dad also had a younger brother, Edward "Hall" Hopple. He married Dorothy and they had a couple of kids. I didn't know them too well as I was off to college, but during my high school years Hall would stop over to our house with a joke or two and we would visit, toss a baseball, etc.

I never knew my maternal grandparents. My grandfather Edwards Ritchie died when I was three. I was named after him. Dad's name was William Andrew Hopple III . . . and he hated the numbers so I wasn't William . . . My paternal grandparents I knew and loved. William A. Hopple, Jr. and Nana. I guess there are a lot of Nana's . . . and I had one. They lived in Wyoming and we saw them often. They would go to the movies with us, and got to Underwood a few times when the family started vacationing there in the summers. At this writing, I still do.

The Farm . . . The Ritchie side of the family had a farm about 10 miles away. All the Ritchies would go there on the Fourth of July for a picnic. They would take homemade beer, fly homemade box kites (really big ones), the kids would ride a pony and explore the barn. (Incidentally, Al Capone rented the barn to store booze in during Prohibition. I don't know whether any of the family knew it.) It was at the farm that a chicken pecked at me and I have disliked birds since then. The food was good, and old farmer "George", who watched the place, was a character. Mom was telling him about the homogenized, golden Guernsey, Vitamin D milk we were getting. He told her that you can't get any better milk than the cow gives. The farm is gone, but I always liked the farm and looked forward to seeing it, as did sister Sal!

Miscellaneous Stuff I Remember about School and WW2 days . . . things were rationed, like butter, meat, gasoline, liquor etc. My Dad got ration cards for all the non-drinkers so they could get a fifth a month (for medicinal purposes as Nana and Aunt Ann would say). We got 4 gallons of gas a week . . . and pooled rides. Dad got a laundry lady and part-time cook because Mom was sick and weak. Mom told the laundry lady, Rose, that we were somewhat grounded. The next Monday when she came she gave Mom a 100-gallon coupon. Don't know where she got it, but I think they gave it to our filling station guy, Ned Blackwood. I guess that gave him an edge. ** We had the groceries delivered from Haller's grocery store. That made it easy on Mom. Every once in a while there was an extra pound of butter in the delivery. ** We would go to Wichman's meat market across the tracks in Lockland to get spareribs for the Memphis Style rib roasts that the family was famous for having. There was a big painted Piggy Tub where you threw the bones. If you missed you didn't get any dessert. ** I collected old newspapers (which were recycled) at a number of homes. I would store them in the closed patio. When the coal man came to deliver coal, I would pitch them into the truck and he would take it back to the company . . . they handled that stuff too. It was a cheap and easy way to help the war and I would earn some spending money.

Friends Dick Smith, Bob Kramig, Bob Taylor, and I would set pins at the Civic Center bowling alley. The Women's League was short pinboys, so they talked the school into letting us out the last period to go set pins. The bowling was candle pins . . . small balls . . . three tries. If the ladies yelled at us, we would set the pins back a little to get even. I don't think they ever knew. ** I did a shoeshine business in grade school and junior high . . . The "Spit-a-Bit" shoe company had mostly family clients. Same with the ice cream freezer. It was a hand-cranked freezer that we hooked a motor on and took it to anyone who wanted us to freeze homemade ice cream . . . for a price.

When the war was over, Dad and I went to buy a new family car. We were getting a Buick Super. The salesman asked him for something down, and he opened his wallet and handed him a dollar bill. The salesman didn't know what to do . . . so he let it slide. Dad paid cash, as always.

We used to go to the Emory Theater in adjacent Reading . . . Riding the bus and seeing the matinee plus the "serial" was an adventure. ** The Stearns & Foster baseball games were fun (the umpire would call an uncaught ball in center field foul for the winning team). ** We used to go to Sharon Woods for picnics, and watch the gliders land and take off at the local airport. ** The gang had Knothole passes for the Reds at Crosley Field ($2 a year, I think). Dick Smith (Smitty) and I would go to an afternoon game, then sneak up the third-base side to Mr. Crosley's box. Powel Crosley owned the Reds. Powel's brother Lewis was always at the game . . . and I knew him because they had come to Underwood a few times as guests of the Dwights. I would say "Hi Mr. Crosley" and the red-coated ushers would swarm. Mr. Crosley would say that's OK and invite us to sit in his box (16 seats . . . maybe 5 people). We found that much more comfortable than the bleachers . . . and the price was right!

I also got to see the first major league *night* game . . . at Crosley Field, May 24, 1935. The Reds beat the Phillies 2 to 1. ** I also saw the Negro league play when the Reds were out of town . . . The Kansas City Clowns vs. St. Louis. It was a Sunday and the players did a tricky routine between the double header games . . . and it was better than the Globetrotters . . . it was unbelievable! The great Sachel Paige pitched. He couldn't play in the major leagues because of the color barrier.

During the WW2 years we took the train to Underwood . . . via Albany, New York. There was usually a gang of 6 or 7. There was a funny limo taxi driver who met us in Albany and drove us to Underwood. Where he got the gasoline, I don't know . . . but he did stop between Albany and Underwood in Pottersville as a rest stop. He left for about 15 minutes, and returned to us. When we got in, we saw the gas tank was full. ** Once in a while he would stop by Underwood with a *trunk* load of meat packed in ice. The Club members bought it all. It beat rationing!

When I was 14 my Dad made me a proposition. Don't drink or smoke until you're 20 and I'll give you a thousand dollars or a Chevy convertible (they were about $800 then). On my 20th birthday I received a check for $1000 with the comment that he didn't want to be found wanting when weighed and hoped it was OK with me if he took the option (Chevy convertibles were about $3000 then). I used the money to start College Radio Corporation and I was off and running.

As a freshman I was on the football team. It was during the war, and our football coach, Bill Jerkovic had gone into the military. Mr. Grimes was our coach, and his expertise was in basketball. We didn't win many games. At that time, players played offense and defense . . . and if you were taken out, you couldn't go back in the game until the next quarter. I played center and linebacker. Most teams used the single wing offense. ** In the baseball season I played catcher on the high school team and we did a little better. ** In Junior High our grade would organize a baseball game on Saturdays to play the next grade. It was fun . . . like intramural games today.

Dad took me to the 1939 World Series where the Reds got hammered by the Yankees in four straight. We had good seats because a friend of Dad's printed the return envelopes for the ticket sales. If you had a permanent box, you got *green* envelopes. We didn't, but used stolen envelopes to apply for tickets, and we got good seats.

I remember sitting around the radio on December 7, 1941 . . . The family, Uncle Hall and some of his friends (Ralph Brown, Gordon Blackwood, Freddie Dewey) and some of my friends were there. We heard FDR's famous address, and other network coverage. A couple of Hall's friends didn't come back.

I had a job at Vedder's Drug Store my senior year. I delivered prescriptions, worked the soda fountain etc. We could eat all we wanted, and I loaded up after my shift for the first week or two. Then it tapered off to almost nothing.

During the war we had "Round Up" at the Wyoming Civic Center where parents and teachers gave us a place to dance and get together. It was the same Civic Center where we set bowling pins . . . and where we took dancing lessons from Madam Fedorova (with piano player Cox) . . . also the venue where I was hat check guy for the New Year's Eve parties. They were held in the same room where, during the war days, women folded bandages for the troops. Smitty and I helped make the folding apparatus (with duct tape and masonite).

It didn't snow much in the Cincinnati area, but when it did we used to go to the golf course to sled. The best sledding, however, was behind Les Webb's car . . . that was fun. He was too. The Webbs were good friends of Mom and Dad. They played cards, and the women played Mah-Jongg and did jigsaw puzzles in the afternoons. Marg Webb was a soft-spoken lady who was unlucky enough to be born on Christmas. She came to Underwood with us and was the den mother in the bunkhouse.

On a special occasion Dad would take us (maybe some others) to Beverly Hills Country Club in Kentucky. It was a great food and nightclub place that had illegal gambling in the big back room. We saw some great shows, including Desi and Lucy, Jimmy Durante, Sophie Tucker, the Glenn Miller Band, Joe E. Lewis, Tony Martin, Duke Ellington, a chorus line, and a great number of Vegas-like acts. It was bigtime stuff. During the war, liquor was rationed. When you went to Beverly Hills you would have an entry on your dinner check for asparagus for $140.00. Dad would pay it, never look in the trunk of the car until we got home, and there would be a case of bourbon pints in the trunk. It filled the gap.

The family would go on short vacations to French Lick, Indiana and Mitawonga on Lake Erie before we went to Underwood in 1938. When I was 6 or 7 they let me run the outboard motor boat we rented at French Lick. I couldn't go far, so I landed it about 100 times, and then took off in a little circle. I loved it and it kept me occupied while they swam or played cards. While Mom was sick and I was about 6, Uncle Herb and Aunt Helen Ritchie took me to Middle Bass Island (on Lake Erie) where they went for a vacation. It was a week-long adventure for me. Their friend Col. Macabee had a 72-foot sailboat . . . and they took me out one afternoon on Lake Erie. We were becalmed and they joked that it was my big ears holding us back. When I stuck chewing gum behind them and tucked them in, we started going. Maybe they were right!

During my high school years I started playing tenor saxophone. Smitty played alto sax, and Kramig played clarinet. We played in the concert band, and we formed a school dance band. It was the Big Band sound, with stock orchestrations. Our teacher, Mr. Letzler, played trombone in the Clyde Trask Orchestra in Cincinnati. We did well with 4 saxes, 3 trumpets, 3 trombones, piano, drums, and bass. We played a lot of school dances, and once in a while one of us would play with other school bands for concerts when their band instructor was short a saxophone etc. It was fun, and I took mine to college and played a little there.

The day after high school graduation my parents invited *Mr. Robert Hecht* for dinner. Mr. Hecht was called "International Robert" by the gang at Stearns and Foster. He was from Atlanta and was in the cotton business. He was an Austrian, very smart, very sloppy, and a great guy. As I was about to go out for the evening, he handed me a $5 bill as a graduation present. When he got back to Atlanta, he sent me a copy of John Gunther's "Inside USA." He wrote in it . . . something like . . . "from an outsider who thinks this is the greatest country in the world." When I had gone to Underwood with the family and friends, he called my Dad and asked if Edwards would like to drive him around the country. We were visiting the Thomsons at Squirrel Island, Maine, when my Dad called and asked if I wanted to do it. My mother really encouraged it. I said "yes", went back to Cincinnati and my Aunt Clem (Memaw) got me packed and clothed. Mr. Hecht showed up in a brand new 1948 blue Cadillac convertible (*first* with the fins) and I was on my way for a seven-week adventure that widened my world and changed my life.

Mr. Hecht and his wife were great to me . . . taught me plenty, and I think he was the most important "Y" in my life. (Incidentally, when Dad was 100 we were talking and he said that he had caught lots of hell from office cohorts for letting me go with Mr. Hecht.) Details of that trip are in Section Two of this book, if you ever get to it.

There were high school fraternities, and I joined ADK . . . and at the initiation I met some other guys from different high schools. Our initation was in Mathew's Woods in Wyoming. I found some guy who wanted to hide until it quieted down, so we found a bunker of sorts. It was Tony Trabert, who later became a tennis icon. ** A few of us guys were coaxed into going to Cotillion in Cincinnati. It was formal and all had to dress to the 9's. None of us liked it, so we spent time shooting dice in the restroom. Smitty called it right when asked how we liked it. He said ". . . there was a men's game in the craproom."

Most of our 40-odd high school graduates went to college. Kramig went to Vanderbilt, Smitty went to Cornell, I went to Amherst, a few went to Miami of Ohio, etc. I chose Amherst because my mom thought I should go to a small liberal arts college . . . she had attended Smith College until she was kicked out for smoking. She said it was a nice small school, so I applied and was accepted. I've never regretted Mom's good advice.

At Christmas when we were young, Santa Claus brought the Christmas tree and some presents. Dad suggested that I leave Santa a beer instead of cookies and milk . . . which I wasn't sure about . . . but I did. **They wrapped the bottom of the tree with a couple of our white cotton furnace filters. Mom sprinkled sparkles on it. A day or so later he implied that S&F could make that Christmas cotton. I think Mom invented it, because you see it all over now.

My hormones must have kicked in a little early, because in kindergarten or first grade I liked a southern belle . . . Marjorie Arthur. She moved away when I was in first grade. In sixth grade I associated with Lois Giese, and in high school with Pat Muir. Pat was in our class of 1948, and at our 40th Reunion we had fun talking about old times. **I headed off to Amherst by train in September 1948, my world having been widened by my seven week trip around the USA and Canada with Mr. Hecht. I had no idea what to expect when I got off the train. I didn't know a soul, but was motivated to plow on!

Pat Muir, high school girlfriend with me and my first car, a 193?
Ford convertible.

ERH at two years old in my Irish mail—note the license plate,
"Repeal Prohibition."

The Las Vegas Flamingo in 1948, when Vegas was new.

A big lobster in Maine—I was 13.

Catching a bass from New Pond at Underwood. It was 1940.

"School Days . . . 1948-49"

Mom's friends Miss Williams,
my Latin teacher, and Marion Maisch,
also a Latin Teacher.

Sister Sally . . . 1948

Yours truly at about age 6+or-.   Mom with her first Underwood bass,
Circa 1940.

Mom's gang of Wyoming gals.

My Uncle Hall Hopple, his college picture.

Dad, Sal, me and Mom—about 1937.

Smitty and me at 40 Linden Drive.

Living Room at Underwood—1940.

Young sister Sal fishing in Nokomis Pond at Underwood—
circa 1938.

Chapter 2 . . . LEAVING THE NEST

Arriving at Amherst College in September 1948 . . . I didn't know anyone, but a couple of possible classmates were on the train. A greeting group met the train in Northampton, Massachusetts and took us by bus the 8 miles to Amherst. We were taken to our dormitory and we found our rooms. There were two new freshman dormitories . . . James and Stearns. I roomed in Stearns (ATW they have been torn down . . . how time flies!). When I got to my room my other three roommates were there, putting their stuff away. They all lived relatively close, so they got there early. Skeet Ellis was from Plymouth, Mass; Brad Wellman was from the Boston area; and Tom Nelson was from Connecticut. We got along well. The next day we went to town to get whatever we needed and get our red freshman beanies. Upper classmen were beginning to arrive and the hat identified the new boys? . . . men? . . . on the block. (Amherst was all male then!) That night there was a freshman get together in the downstairs recreation room. We met other guys from the different floors, and the group impressed me. I met Bob Vance, who was a chaperon for Stearns Dorm. You'll see his name throughout this book. This is where I first met him, and we've been partners and friends ever since.

Curriculum, Faculty, and Things Academic . . . The class of 1948 was the first year of what the college called the New Curriculum. All freshmen had to take it. It was inventive and very broad . . . real liberal artsy. There were basically "areas" of study. One was "Physics I," where during the year we dabbled in statistics, calculus, physics, and chemistry. Maybe biology was in there too, but I've since found out in life that it isn't "exact." Another area was "The Humanities" where we had classes in the ancient and modern literature, read and wrote about many of them . . . and dabbled twice a week in the infamous "English One." In that course you wrote a paper for every class. The whole English Department worked with this course, and many years later they discontinued it because they said that they didn't quite know what they were doing. I'm not sure I did either! It taught crazy semantics . . . something like . . . A basket is a chair if you sit on it. You are the total result of your environment . . . maybe not total . . . but if you go to town down Street A instead of Street B, you'll see different things and it will affect your life henceforth. (Tough to prove.)

Another area had to do with history, which consisted of three weekly lectures. In the first few weeks the Geology dept. established the planet. I think the Religious dept. put people and/or animals on it. Then some lectures about ancient civilizations, the Geography Dept. got the continents and countries in order at various lectures along the line . . . and the various history departments took us from BC to May, 1949. The last lecture of the year was from that day's NY Times. The wars . . . politics . . . leaders . . . the civilizations . . . religions . . . trends and dominances were all given by dynamic professors. The leader of the profs was Prof Laurence Packard . . . maybe Lawrence . . . but he was great! His lecture on the Battle of Jutland lasted longer than the battle. It was so famous that the lecture hall was jammed with other teachers, alumni, town folks, and others who had heard about it. Quite a show! This class had papers to write, and special books printed about subjects like: "The Turner Thesis" (rugged individualism etc.) or "Rockefeller—Industrialist or Robber Baron." You picked a side and wrote a paper defending your position.

Damn if I can remember if or what another academic area was. In addition we had P.E., an elective such as Music or Art, and a choice of languages. I took Spanish. My first semester I received the only "D" I ever got. (Hard to believe that I ultimately owned Spanish Language Radio Stations, and was a big factor in the development of Spanish Radio as a big business. I was Daniel Boone in that growth.)

I had Colston E. Warne for an Economics Professor. He was liberal but he was fair. I wrote a paper on the National Association of Manufacturers and received an "A" . . . but I'm sure he had no use for the organization. He was the first President of the newly formed Consumers Union. When he came to class you could hear him shut the door of his Plymouth 10 or 12 times . . . presumably checking for quality or weaknesses.

I also had Robert Frost for a twice a week English class in my junior or senior year . . . not sure which. At that time they took attendance at the classes, and you were allowed a cut for every hour. I happened to be sitting in the front row, and he asked if I would take attendance. I said "Yes" and he turned to the class and said "If you come to class, you'll get a C. Why should I fail you? Let life fail you!"

About the third week he said that he would not be there the next class. He had to go to NYC to record for the Voice Of America. He added . . . "it's easier to do than explain why I don't want to do it." Frost talked about his buddy Carl Sandburg, etc. At one lecture someone (who studied all the time) asked what it meant between the lines in his poem ". . . miles to go before I sleep . . ." He said it didn't have any underlying meaning . . . that he was tired and he wanted to go home. ** Frost spent a semester at Dartmouth and one at Amherst those years. The Amherst Library is named for him, and was dedicated by John F. Kennedy a few months before he was shot. During the semester he was at Amherst he would visit each fraternity or Club in the evening for a couple of hours. They always had a professor following . . . or leading . . . him around. If they lost him, he would be out in a nearby tobacco field with his dog talking to the farmer.

In one 14th century French History class, I had not done the reading and was cramming at the library for the midterm exam scheduled in about one hour. A friend of mine, Mark Weber, had it down pat (he said). He gave a mini verbal synopsis right there in the library. We took the blue book exam. The next meeting the professor said that many had gotten the gist of the times and then he read one paper which he said summed it up very well. It wasn't until he handed out the papers that I realized it was mine. Easy come . . . easy go! All in all, I graduated with a BA . . . and was a B—student. Most of that was due to the fact that I spent too many hours with extracurricular activities.

About Those Extracurricular Activities that got in the way of studying . . .
When I went to college, my Dad told me that he would support it so I wouldn't have to sling hash and would have time to socialize and study. (I later found out he graduated from Kenyon cum laude). He strongly suggested that I do things for experience rather than concentrate on sports . . . or music . . . such as working for the student newspaper, yearbook, etc. I took his advice . . . maybe too much . . . because I felt slightly un-academic. ** My freshman year John Lancaster (an upper classman) and I did a football pool.

We printed cards, peddled them . . . tallied them and figured if three teams won it would hurt us, so we bet on them at the local (bookie) florist. That was hedging other people's bets! **My first adventure was in the business section of The Amherst Student, the campus newspaper. I sold ads, developed affinity groups to share an ad, and helped in the distribution of the paper . . . including mailing copies to subscribers, like parents, alumni, etc. I was made National Advertising Manager the second semester of my sophomore year. We were represented by National Advertising Service in New York. I got a form letter congratulating me and inviting me to come to visit them in NYC. Very few did, but I did. I saw desks full of old college newspaper checking copies and very few people. I liked that. I was told it was owned by W. B. Bradbury and Madison Sayles . . . they each worked a week on and a week off. Word hath it they met at noon on Wednesdays at the Harvard Club and passed the "scoop" to the oncoming guru. I REALLY liked that!

At times I worked for the humor magazine and the OLIO, the Amherst yearbook . . . but most of my time was consumed in developing the wired-wireless radio station on campus, WAMF. Somehow I found time to work with the football team, and earned a letter my senior year as Manager. Along the way I got into Phi Delta Theta Fraternity, and the Sphinx (Jr. year) and Scarab (Sr. year) honor societies. It was quite an honor, but I don't think they exist now. And don't forget . . . we had to go to Chapel three days a week . . . or know the attendance taker.

About the Campus Radio Station . . . WAMF . . . It was a new wired wireless AM campus radio station. That means the signal came through the electric system and somehow Bob Vance got it into all the college buildings . . . DIIK how. (It is now a non-commercial Educational FM station.) We secured space in the basement of Walker Hall, built studios, and broadcast eight hours a day. The Student Council gave us a budget which we immediately overspent. That's not good, and they told us so in certain terms. I never liked budgets, and still don't. It was a very minor extracurricular activity in most of the college peoples' eyes. The turning point was when we secured a 24-hour INS News teletype printer at the station. We talked INS (International News Service—no longer around) into service for some $15 a week and hiatus when school was out. The word got out and professors came down, football players, even the President, Charlie Cole, came down to see the automatic typewriter spit out breaking news.

Many students decided they would like to be associated with WAMF and we had a staff. Phil Kolodner started a weekly 15-minute Walter Winchell type show on Wednesday nights. He got his scoop from around campus or made it up, but it had listeners galore. My good friend to this day, Phil Knowles did a show, and helped Vance et al put together a lined network with Smith College, The University of Masachusetts, and American International College in Springfield. We had connecting phone lines, Western Union clocks that set themselves every hour, interchange of programs, and publicity on the campuses. We called it The Pioneer Broadcasting System. It was the first line connected collegiate radio network in the country. We built a great music library, and a bunch of the student staff went on to work at radio production and then on into TV. It was Knowles' and Vance's baby.

Living at the Phi Delta Theta House . . . My junior year I moved into the Phi Delt house. There were about 30 guys living there . . . and we got along well. Most of the members would bring girls in on Friday and Saturday night, usually from Smith or Mt. Holyoke colleges. We had beer in the bar, and gals had to be out by eleven sharp!

Eddie Davenport was our custodian. He was also a trainer for the football team, and one of the neatest guys I have ever met. ** Someone always had an idea of how to waste time, so we would take a road trip to Boston to go to the burlesque shows . . . The Casino and Old Howard in Scully Square. They're gone now, which is probably good. We made trips to the horse races at Revere Beach near Boston . . . maybe it was dogs! Occasionally . . . or maybe more often . . . we would go to Springfield to the Hub. It was a bar that gave you change in silver dollars. I wish I had saved some! There was always a group that would go to a couple of the favorite watering holes in Northampton, Holyoke, Greenfield, and to Barselotti's, the Amherst home of legendary waitress Lil. She wore about 20 fraternity pins. ** During this period I started dating Margie Cramer, who was a freshman at Smith College. She was a beautiful gal and neat person from St. Louis. We had some great times together.

Also during my senior year, Bob Vance and I rented an office over the Amherst Book Store. Maybe it was the theater. Anyway we started the College Radio Corporation business there . . . at least we found out how many college radio stations there were by mailing a questionnaire to a list of 1200+ colleges. We got little response! Vance or I came up with the idea of sending another questionnaire stating we were doing a paper on the subject. We asked if whoever received it would pass it on to the proper person. We addressed them to the President of the College. That got results! We ended up with about 100 stations.

Some Memorable Vacations and breaks during my college days (1948-1952) . . . I went home for Christmas my first year and found that Mom and Dad had a first TV set . . . two hours a day, mostly news and boxing. Dad said he wished he had bought Philco stock instead of the set. It was early in TV'S history. My second-year Christmas vacation was great. My sister Sal worked for American Airlines in the Reservations dept. in Cincinnati. She and Mom had worked out a free week's trip on American Airlines for her and me, starting the day after Christmas, to Camelback Inn in Phoenix, Arizona. We were on standby, but it didn't make any difference. Sal's cohorts in the reservation dept. knew she was going, and filled other flights. When we got onto the plane there were about eight other people going to Dallas. (No trouble on to Phoenix either.) It was a terrific resort, very personal, and had some very nice people. I thought Sal should see Las Vegas . . . my having been there with Mr. Hecht. We flew Bonanza Airlines to Las Vegas for one night . . . stayed at the Sands. They would cash a check for anybody for $100, so I cashed a check. They sent me a credit card after I got home. That card made a big difference . . . as the book will point out later.

We got home and I went back to Amherst to continue college. My junior Thanksgiving vacation was a hoot. A bunch went to NYC. Storms were horrible. Fraternity brother Ted Nugent lived in the city, and there was a big . . . I mean *big* . . . coming-out party at the Pierre Hotel. They were desperate to find dates because those coming from other colleges couldn't get there because of the terrible weather. Ted and I (maybe more) were enlisted to substitute. I had a black suit . . . which was lucky . . . but they were so desperate that you could come in a bathing suit and be accepted. Before the event we were invited to a townhouse on Park Avenue. Alice Blue was the gal's name, and the joint was outrageous. Doormen, butlers, waitresses, just like the movies. Her parents were very nice to us, hoping we wouldn't duck out. The actual party was very nice . . . the best of everything . . . and at the end the parents thanked us profusely. It was a great gig! **I saw a couple of Broadway shows on that trip too . . . . South Pacific, Pal Joey, etc.

On Spring Break my junior year a bunch drove to Fort Lauderdale. The only person that we could use as a contact was the bartender at the Seacrest Manor in Hollywood, Florida. Three or four cars went, stopping different places, and my car finally got to the bartender to log our different locations. Frank and Jan Tindle were there . . . and they asked where we were from. We told them Amherst. They asked if we knew Hoyte Long. We told him he was a fraternity brother of ours. They bid good night, but I think Cathie's mother made her stay down in the bar. About ten minutes later there was a call for her in the bar. It was her father asking if we wanted to come to dinner the next day. We said yes. The four of us went to dinner the following day . . . and Frank told us that long ago he had come from Dartmouth to Florida for a Spring Break . . . short of funds . . . and felt we were probably in the same boat. He was right. At dinner we decided to go to the horse races the following day. Cathie and some other gals staying there went with us. We lost our $2 a race, but Cathie came informed. Her mother had called the house bookie, Zeke, at the Seacrest and he gave her some good tips. Cathie won! All in all, it was a memorable week . . . and obviously influenced my life.

Later, I saw Cathie, who was then going to Bradford Junior College, at the Amherst Phi Delt House. She was a weekend date of fraternity brother Jack Orr. I'd later meet Cathie in Buffalo . . . at a beach party . . . and I asked her if she wanted to go to the races. She did . . . we did . . . and that was the beginning of our relationship. My sister Sal and I went to Buffalo to Cathie's coming-out party, and we were entertained royally.

Summer of 1952 between Graduation and Grad School . . . Somehow, after taking tests and interviews I was accepted at Harvard Biz School and Law School in the same mail! I still don't know why. Bob Vance and I had come up with a scheme to represent College Radio Stations. Knowing what the INS machine did for WAMF, we told the stations, who were skeptical of who we were and what we would do for them, that the answer would be "nothing . . . OR we would put a news machine in their station and they would pay nothing . . . just give us a daily 15-minute newscast to utilize for National commercials. It seemed fair to us . . . and to some 90 stations. They really had nothing to lose. We had to sell the newscast package, administer it, and save something for ourselves, We went to NYC and stayed at the George Washington Hotel on 23rd Street. (They gave Amherst people a deal.) We contacted the Lucky Strike Cigarette account executives at BBDO. Trying to look professional, we took one to lunch. He said they were interested, but didn't see how anyone could do it for what we were asking for the yearly package. They were right, but we solved it by doubling the price. They bought it, and we were rolling.

Fall of 1952 I enrolled at Harvard Law School . . . and roomed at 66 Oxford Street in Cambridge. There were six of us. It was interesting, but I wasn't enthralled. Most of the professors wrote the books we used. We joined a "fraternity" eating place there, and took a few memorable trips. One night eight of us went to see H. M. S. Pinafore. Dick Button of ice skating fame was with us. He commented how graceful the dancers were . . . and here's a man that did things on ice that no one had ever done. Afterwards we decided to make an evening of it and see Tony Bennett at a night club. We did, and a bunch of the guys asked some gals to dance. I was the only one left, and there was one gal at their table too. I decided to ask her to dance. When we sat down after the music stopped, the gang told me I better get in shape. They said I was dancing with Rocky Marciano's wife. He was away training. I didn't believe them until I saw her leave in a big car with Massachusetts license plate "KO." ** On other trips we would go to Durgin Park to eat. Great food . . . all you could eat . . . surly waitresses . . . and you ate in the kitchen. It's still great 55 years later. During the election, Ike Eisenhower came through Cambridge and I shook his hand. The only thing we had in common was we were Republicans and both liked Wild Turkey. I joined the Harvard Coop. I drank green beer on St. Patrick's day, and learned a little something. I had five academic draft deferrals, and it would take some doing to get more. I decided I would go into the draft if I could get an exemption for a few months to finish the College Radio thing. I did. Vance was doing the work in Columbus, Ohio . . . administration was tough . . . and I sold a few accounts in NYC on College Radio. I stayed at the Biltmore Hotel . . . a room with a path (to the bath) . . . for $3 a night. Under the clock at the Biltmore was a famous meeting place.

Fun and Work for a few months in NYC . . . before the Army . . . The College Radio Corp. office was a desk at 545 Fifth Avenue. That was a crazy group of people, but I met some interesting people in those four or five months. Bill Irvine, John Murphy, Peggy Lumpkin, Marty Rokeach, and Dave Crow were among them. Cathie had graduated from Bradford Jr. College and was going to Tufts. She came from Boston to NYC almost every weekend . . . stayed in another $3 room at the Biltmore. We saw shows, went to jazz joints, and "did" the Big Apple. Time went by and I went home to

Cincinnati for Christmas . . . and entered the draft in January, 1954. Bill Irvine and I had started a P.I. business. We contacted a list of commercial radio stations that took P.I. advertising (Per Inquiry). P.I. meant that the broadcast station got paid by the number of orders they received from listeners. We got 8 or 10 radio stations to air The Blade Man commercials . . . a box of 100 razor blades for $14.95. The station would take $5 from the money . . . we would buy the blades for about $3.00. We sent them out and made $5 for each order. Another item we had was the "Connie Mac Baseball Book" which we bought from "Remainders" for about a buck. Same kind of split with the stations. I'm not sure about the numbers, but I assume you get the idea. We did OK! The Westover, Massachusetts station did the best of all the stations. Mike Burns, who worked as a messenger for Irvine, would pick up the products on his rounds . . . saved us time and money.

The Army . . . Buck Private . . . and I did make Corporal . . . On January 9, 1954 I was bused to Fort Knox, Kentucky, for basic training. It was cold. On arrival we were given a flying $20 . . . then off to the barber shop, where the floor was *full* of hair. The long-hairs were pissed when they got crew cuts. I guess I got in some kind of physical shape. We had to take an Officers' Training School exam. It was a slam dunk, but trying to explain why I didn't want to go was not! They pestered me through basic training to go to OTS. I wanted none of it. Then we took typing tests. Out of high school I could do about 50 words a minute. I backed down to 25-30 words per minute. I wanted to go to clerk typist school, so I wanted to do well enough to get that chance, but not too well . . . or too badly. I made it and that was also eight weeks at Fort Knox. They talked about AG stenography school at Fort Benjamin Harrison, in Indianapolis, Indiana. I liked that because it was close to Cincinnati, and I could go home. Mom wasn't doing too well. I decided to move my speed up to qualify for that school, and it was easy by then. At the end of clerk typist school, I was ordered to the AG Stenography School. ** Steno School was a blast. Good food. No KP! Just 8 hours a day of typing and learning shorthand.

In the mix was English of all kinds . . . spelling, grammar, structure, punctuation etc. There were civilian instructors. We could leave post every night. We would go into Indianapolis and sneak into Eli Lilly's private residence pool. The caretakers didn't care, and when someone was there . . . we would leave. I got to go home a number of weekends, which was nice. On "campus" there was a classmate who came from Las Vegas.

The Commanding Officer allowed him to run a very low stakes blackjack game in the barracks. I'm not sure why! His name was Don Dobson, and he was a major "Y" in my road. I had my "Sands Hotel" card (previously mentioned), which impressed him. He allowed me to give him checks (they were small) . . . which he sent to his mother in Las Vegas. After eighteen weeks of study we all graduated.

My orders said to Vietnam. I was going to get married soon and that assignment didn't fit in my plans. By luck I found a classmate who had been assigned to Fort Bragg, North Carolina. He lived there in Fayetteville where Fort Bragg is located. He wanted to go overseas, so I suggested we could switch. We went to the enlisted man in the AG section and told him what we would like to do. He said he didn't care, and switched the orders. I was on my way to the XVIII Airborne Corps at Fort Bragg. Dobson and I had gotten to know each other pretty well. We even took a road trip to the racetrack in Chicago. It was his suggestion. We had a good time but his "tips" were not good. On the way home the six passengers had about $4 among us. Before we all left Benjamin Harrison, I told Don Dobson that if something ever came up in Las Vegas . . . an opportunity of sorts . . . that I had friends and we could probably raise some cash to participate. Evidently he didn't forget that comment, because a couple of years later he called me in NYC (we were both out of the Army). He introduced me to the Tahoe Biltmore deal.

Fort Bragg, North Carolina . . . a stenographer in the XVIII Corps AG section . . . and even a Private First Class . . . There were quite a few in my barracks who had been to jump school. There were bars on the windows so they would not get to dreaming and jump out. The office was interesting, and employed many civilians. The AG section handled Orders . . . shipped people all over the world . . . and handled the clerical part of jumping 50,000 men a week. My mother died in November while I was there, and I got emergency leave to go home. Her passing was probably a blessing. After the funeral, Dad took me to the airport to return to Fayetteville. We were busy talking about a number of things and the plane left without me. Imagine this. There was another plane 20 minutes later, and I got to Fayetteville before the plane that I missed.

I married the *Love* of my life . . . Catharine Lulu Thomas . . . in Buffalo, NY, on April 16, 1955 . . . It was a beauteous camp meet. Many people came from Cincinnati, and I appreciated their coming mucho miles for the festivities. The out-of-towners stayed at the Buffalo Country Club where we had the rehearsal party. Dad was alone, so he brought good friend Tommy Lloyd to do his drinking for him. Great choice! Great party! Bishop Scaffe (a friend of Cathie's grandfather "Bobbie") wouldn't marry anyone until they had talked to him. He liked us, and we were OK. The church was full. The Bishop had four weddings that day. He carried a handy dandy case with all the stuff . . . fresh collars, smelling salts, a Bible, and other "man of the cloth" materials. The wedding party was *big* . . . and so was the reception. After we kissed at the ceremony Cathie whispered "Let's get the hell out of here." The limo stopped at the photo shop, which he owned, to get Cathie a pack of cigarettes . . . and then we were off to the Country Club for the reception. It was sit-down and probably 150 people. The Bishop told Cathie that he enjoyed her comment . . . and repeated it. She didn't know what to say. ** We left in the new black Chevrolet convertible that her parents had given us. Dad matched it with equal Cash. A very nice start. We spent the first night at the Auburn Inn. Three years later, when Dad and Janet were on their honeymoon, they stopped there too. Dad told the desk clerk that his son had enjoyed his honeymoon there so they thought they would try it. The next night we spent in Williamsburg, Virginia . . . and then on to Myrtle Beach, South Carolina, for a few days. We headed back to Fayetteville and our little house. My barber had built a $2000 house . . . really . . . and it almost had wall-to-wall floors. Cathie loved it . . . that may be an overstatement. It was neat for us and married Army life was on the way.

New York City . . . 1956 World Series . . . new office . . . I got a leave and Cathie and I went to NYC to see College Radio's new office in the Chrysler Building. We also got World Series tickets and watched brother-in-law Rip Coleman pitch against the Brooklyn Dodgers at Ebbetts Field. Later Rip told me that he wondered why he ever thought pitching for the Yankees in a World Series was going to be so great. We updated and saw many of our friends. Five days seemed like a day . . . then back to the grind at Fort Bragg.

About the Army AG Section work . . . if you could call that work . . . I was a Bird Colonel's so-called secretary. He was a neat guy and we got along well. One time he had to make a speech for a service club. He asked me what he should talk about. I told him to talk about something he knew something about (which limited his subject matter). I suggested getting in some one liners to keep the audience awake. I dug in the Readers Digest and found a bunch. He used them and said they loved his speech. I was in with him! Later I told him that I had to leave to go to Fort Campbell because I was the only steno at Fort Bragg. He told me to give him my file. He erased my Military Occupational Specialty number on the file and changed it to Clerk Typist. There were plenty of them around. A great break for me!

Cathie and I got arrested by an MP for going 28 mph in a 25 mph zone. I told him he didn't want to do that, but he insisted. The next month when the orders came in, I asked the Colonel if I could do the MPs . . . and he said "Sure." We would get a file box of the MPs at Fort Bragg, reach in by chance and pull a file. I reached in by chance (ha!) and got his file. I assigned him to Shape headquarters in Paris. I then called the sergeant who shipped stuff and told him to get this guy's stuff, ship it as slow as possible and let me know when it was all gone. He said he owed me one and would do. When he called me back and said it was gone, I changed the orders to Borneo. Payback on a ticket! I still wonder if he ever got his "stuff."

Fort Bragg had the 72nd Airborne Division, and they all jumped. We had over 50,000 jumps a week. Some were in jump school . . . some were staying qualified so as to get the jump pay. We had everything from privates to generals jumping. I had the Red phone on my desk. When there was a splatter, they would call it in to me and I'd call the Secretary of the Army . . . I'd give the identifying info and they would take it from there. When I first had that assignment, it was spooky answering the Red phone. After a while it was just another case.

Once in a while I would assist the Officer of the Day . . . who had nothing to do. That was easy. ** On the light side, the barracks had a G.I. inspection. The veteran Sergeant told us he wanted everything perfect. He addressed us all and said to be sure there were no holes in our socks. He then asked if there were any questions. I asked "If there are no holes in our socks, how do we get our feet in?" That cost me a week on KP.

KP wasn't bad. The Corps food was very good. At five am we reported to the chief chef. I saw him put coal in a stove and throw 10 pounds of butter in to light it. That's government!

There was a Sgt. Howard Kester running around, and he had heard that I had something to do with radio. When we met, he asked me if I would like to run a TV camera for a weekly show at the newly built TV station . . . the first in Fayetteville. I said "sure." He was the Director. He didn't know much but neither did anyone else around there. There were two cameras, and we pushed them around as directed. The show was a singer and country band. It was adjacent to a radio station . . . where the leading disc jockey's name was Branch Twig. Is that Country Western or what? Later Howie Kester was running the Northern California Broadcasters Association in San Francisco. I was a director of the Southern California Broadcasters Association, so I stopped to see him one day and we laughed about the Army times and people. I think somehow he headed me into some regional business for my stations.

On some weekends Cathie and I would go to Myrtle Beach for R&R. There was one country club there and we joined it for $100. There are probably 100 now. They had some rooms, and we stayed there. Cathie's sister Claire came to see us at Ft. Bragg, and we took her to Myrtle Beach. She wanted to sleep on the floor, so we let her do it. The trouble was that the floors had been recently varnished and she stuck to the floor. It was a hoot.

We got to meet Pat and Jake Hake. He was an enlisted man from Cincinnati and I prevented him from having to go overseas. He was a civilian architect, and years later they bought our house at 40 Linden Drive in Wyoming. Small world! **The Hakes somehow knew a local judge who belonged to the Fayetteville Country Club. We often got to join them for Sunday Buffet, and it made a nice social break. There was a daughter around that gang who wanted to be an actress. Years later Cathie saw her as "Meg" on General Hospital . . . or was it All My Children . . . Cathie's favorite soap opera. ** I met George Mason in the AG section and we became good friends. I think he made sergeant. When he got out, his wife June and he came to help run the Tahoe Biltmore. I was working with George for a major who always went to the officer's club and then came back to sign all the paperwork. I got out of the Army three months early by going to school . . . the Columbia School of Broadcasting in NYC. It was a sham . . . and the GI bill paid for it. My last day I told the Major that I was leaving. He asked who signed the release. I said "you did." He gave me a funny look and then wished me luck in the future. He knew that I had feathered my release paper into his stack one day . . . and he always blindly signed the whole pile on his desk in front of him. I guess that's good enough for government work!

Cathie in her wedding gown, married April 16, 1955

Men in our wedding—April 16, 1955

Cathie and me in NYC, with our apartment in background.

Sister Sal with a fish in Florida.   Marge Cramer, college girl friend.

EDWARDS R. HOPPLE
40 Linden Drive, Wyoming, Cincinnati 15, Ohio
Wyoming High School   *Economics*
ΦΔΘ   Football, "A", Manager; Band; CONTEXT,
Business Manager; Intramural Council; Managerial
Association; OLIO, Treasurer; Pre-Law Club; SA-
BRINA, Business Manager; STUDENT, Circulation
Manager; WAMF, Station Manager; Sphinx; Scarab.

From my Amherst yearbook . . . OLIO 1952.

Stepmother Janet, grandmother Nana and Aunt Ann Anderson.
Circa 1960.

Chapter 3 . . . YOUTHFUL ENTHUSIASM

Off to the Big Apple to "work" . . . Cathie and I left Fort Bragg, our little house, and our military and civilian friends . . . and some great memories! We got to NYC and started hunting for an apartment. We ended up on the 7th floor of 165 E. 35th Street. It was new and on Third Avenue. The elevated was just being torn down, and the part by our building was still up. It didn't last long, though. Between moving in and arriving in NYC we stayed a week at a cheap hotel on the West Side right across from the studio for NBC's Late Night Show with Steve Allen. There was all kinds of noise around 11 pm and 1 am. We laughed at it, while spitting grape seeds across the room. Youth is great!

The College Radio Office was in the Chrysler Building, and it was convenient. We combined with William Rambeau, one of the first radio station reps. He was getting old and needed some spark . . . and some stations. That was called Rambeau, Vance & Hopple, Inc. Rambeau finally retired . . . or Vance kicked him out . . . but whatever happened we decided to move to 14 West 45th Street . . . where the "economic bordello" was born. Space with desks . . . old but neat. I was going to the Columbia School of Broadcasting to fulfill my military obligation. There I met a Jack Davis who knew some stuff about radio engineering. He helped Vance build a broadcast studio at 14 West 45th. Career Magazine was there, John Murphy printing rep, Bill Irvine with Basil Smith Engravings, David Ross Crow Associates (radio production), College Humor Magazine Reps, and other miscellaneous enterprises.

All the people were friends and a little crazy. On December 24th we stopped work at one o'clock and went across the street to the Red Raven for some lunch and some Christmas Cheer before going home. That was the embryo of the *Christmas Lunch* we have yearly to this day. Guys come from all over, although the original "20+" are down to about 6. I'm *glad* I'm one of them! We just had the 56th in New York at the Capital Grill on 42nd street on December 10, 2008.

Weekends and Fun during this time . . . A great number of times Cathie and I would go to her parents' summer home on the Canadian shore (Applegarth) for the weekend. There were other times when we stayed at the Tindles' home in Buffalo. They were neat and they would entertain us . . . and some of our friends. Bob and Nancy Vance and I would come and sail on the Tindles' boat "Duchess." So did my sister Sally and brother-in-law Rip Coleman . . . with daughter Vicki. They'd come to Applegarth when Rip was playing baseball and his team—Montreal or Denver or some such—was playing Buffalo. (Incidentally, Claire Tindle would go to all the games when Rip came to Buffalo.) Cathie would stay in Buffalo the whole week when it was hot and I would go back to New York and play like I was working. When Cathie was in town, we would go to shows, restaurants, movies, and special events and places.

We went to Gettysburg one weekend; Atlantic City (before gambling). Cathie had been there with her grandparents when she was very young. She said it hadn't changed! We went to Vance's house in New Canaan, CT; Boston; and even Cincinnati. Our favorite restaurant was Cherios on 57th Street in NYC. Other joints we frequented were the Blue Angel (where Bob Vance introduced a patron to TV Star Henry Morgan. Strangely enough he didn't know Henry or the patron, but the patron was thrilled. Another Vance-ism!); Eddie Condon's, The Dooley Sisters, The Metropole, Basin Street (Where the Boss knew Vance very well), The Latin Quarter (where a gang including Ma Boo enjoyed the nightclub act while Vance smoked a cigar with the owner in his office . . . one more Vance-ism), and the St. James *after-hours* club. The St. James on E. 61st had a great group of show people, great piano music, and terrific drinks . . . all at moderate prices. After the St. James on weekends we would go to the *Yukon* on Third Avenue for buffalo steak. We got home about 7 am after a night on the town. To finish the weekend we would go to the *Hickory House* on Sunday afternoon to hear great piano players, and then Marty Rokeach would go with us to Chinatown for dinner. All in all we loved the time in NYC.

At the office we did the voice-over for the *Jill Cory Show* on college radio. We would send the college stations the records and a disc with the intro, closing, commercials (Old Gold Cigarettes) and the in-between talk. I guess we sent instructions too! The scripts were written by Steve Sondheim. He got $5 a show, and would stop by the office to get a check . . . so he could eat. He was collaborating with Leonard Bernstein on West Side Story. His success on Broadway is a legend. He wrote a theme for the Cory show and charged us $200.00. We often wonder if it showed up later in one of his many successful Broadway musicals. Vance lost our copy . . . a Vance-ism again.

The College Radio newscast plan was on almost 100 college stations. Lucky Strike Cigarettes sponsored it. The people at BBDO advertising agency and the American Tobacco Company were very cooperative . . . and especially Chet Jackson and Fritz Wilhelmi from American Tobacco, Marty Rokeach and Tax Cummings from the ad agency, and Carl Molander of United Press. **At the "economic bordello" (14 W 45th in NYC) we had a great time with all the businesses. Some made it and some didn't (both people and businesses).

It was a fateful Monday morning when the gang arrived at the office. Each guy had a "deal" offered to him/her over the weekend. John Murphy was offered something from millionaire playboy Bainton (A college acquaintance, or close). Bill Irvine and someone were developing a National College Humor Magazine. Dave Crow was messing with becoming an angel for a Broadway production.

It was my turn at bat and I told the gang that an Army friend of mine called and wanted to put together a group to buy a hotel-casino in Lake Tahoe. Most said "WOW" and asked more about it. I told them that it was at the North end of Lake Tahoe. I had left him (Don Dobson—one of the Y's in my road) at Army steno school with the thought that if anything became available, I might put together a group for some of the action. That was a Hopple-ism! Don had said that we could make the nut on the Fourth of July. He said that if I/we wanted to come out and take a look, he and his partner would meet us and show us around the Tahoe Biltmore.

Crow said he would go; Nancy and Bob Vance would go if they could ski at Squaw Valley (9 miles away); and Cathie said she would go if we could go to Las Vegas. Crow checked with the airlines, and found a flight (TWA—12 hours to San Francisco). We said let's go . . . I told Dobson that we were coming . . . and about when we would be there . . . and the Syndicate from the East was about to be born . . . or airborne . . . in February 1957.

The Beginning of the Tahoe Biltmore Adventure . . . The syndicate gathered at La Guardia . . . settled in and laughed. Chicago was about four hours. We got box lunches in Chicago, had a drink or two and got to San Francisco in the evening. We rented a car and headed to Reno. We stayed overnight someplace, and the next day met Don and his partner (I forget his name because he somehow evaporated and was never in the deal) in Reno. We went to the hotel, not knowing what the hell we were doing. We, as a group, thought it would be fun . . . interesting . . . new and different. Bobby Vernon was the former manager and he had stayed on to watch the place with an eye to connecting with the new owners.

That night we stayed in Reno at the Riverside Hotel and discussed what we could do . . . played some slot machines where Cathie enjoyed getting the radishes (cherries), and threw a couple of Morgan Silver Dollars in the river for good luck. We saw Squaw Valley where the 1960 Winter Olympics were going to be held. I don't know whether the Vances skied or not. Cathie didn't get to Las Vegas because Reno was enough. We all returned to NYC dedicated to getting up the cash to do the deal. Monday at the office there were comments, questions and ideas from everyone.

Arranging Financing . . . I suppose this is the story of my life . . . and still is just that. We corralled Marty Rokeach from BBDO to get some investors, Vance and I used College Radio money, and we hit our parents and friends. My Dad was reluctant, as was Frank Tindle, Mr. Hecht, and many others . . . but we got a bankroll together. It got close to the deadline, so Dave Crow called his mother. She called her banker and they wired $40,000 to the law firm in Los Angeles. We were in business, at least we thought we were.

Vance (who was to remain in NY running the CRC business) came for a little while and did the accounting setup; Marty Rokeach took a leave of absence from BBDO to come out and work; Phil Knowles came out, along with Cathie and me; George Mason, my friend from the Army, and his wife June came out; Dave Crow was there; old manager Bobby Vernon was hired, and we all got there about the middle of June, 1957.

Dobson had leased the casino to a group headed by Jackie Gaughan . . . and Larry Hezzlewood from Las Vegas, Jack (Tiger) Novack from Omaha (Gaughan's partner), and a small group of Damon Runyon characters . . . like Jughead, Claude Favarot, King, Patsy Delulio, et al. To make a long story short, we ran the dining room for 4 weeks and closed it. There were more people in the kitchen than the dining room. Running a hotel, bar, dining room, pool, and other amenities is not easy. We were going downhill . . . and knew it . . . but hung on.

We operated during that winter . . . skeleton gaming crew on weekends when Geramoni Tours brought up skiers. They would have one or two buses . . . . We leased the kitchen . . . but we operated the hotel and the bar. George Mason and I worked the bar. When they checked in, we would hand them a towel, some soap, and a key and point to the room. There were six cabins outside, each with 4-6 rooms. We also used the main hotel building. which had some 25 rooms. We all slept in trailers in the back during summer and on weekends . . . but moved *in* when the crowd left. During the week, one maid did all the rooms. If people happened to come in to rent a room, we would give them their choice of an $18, $22, or $26 room. It was the same room, but they got to choose what they wanted to pay.

The following summer we went bare bones. We sold it to Fitzerald in the fall (when the mortgage holder decided we should pay him). We lost all our investment . . . plus a little time . . . but proudly didn't give any purveyor a haircut!

Cathie and I had our car which Marty Rokeach had driven west. He and Jack Davis drove it across the country nonstop. Jack was there for 2 days, and when I saw him walking over to the California line (maybe 200 yards), I asked him what he was doing. He said that when he got back East, if anyone asked him if he'd been to California . . . he could say "seven or eight times".

Cathie and I drove back to NYC through Las Vegas (she finally got there), and had a nice trip. I was on my way back to Madison Avenue to sell time at Rambeau, Vance Hopple. On that trip I stopped at KENO in Las Vegas and signed them up to represent them for advertising in New York. They had *no* National business. That is when I first met Jan and Gordon Sherwood. I had worked hard, and although not successfully, Jackie Gaughan saw and liked Cathie and me. Two months later he called me and asked if I would like to be Advertising Manager at the Flamingo in Las Vegas. That's another story to come. (I was to become sixth in line for that job, which started with Buggsy Siegel).

In Tahoe . . . we had some funny things happen. ** Cathie and June Mason ran the cigarette machine, the juke box, and the pinball machine. They bought the cigarettes in California, and used the profits to have fun. They had fingernail polish on quarters which the bar and juke box used. When the owner came, he would give those back to them and split the profit.

In the winter the skiers would party Saturday night. On Sunday morning some priest would set up the blackjack table in the casino as a place to have Mass. George and I would close the bar while we went from saloon to synagogue and back again. One time we went upstairs to the linen room to take a leak and there was a priest in there taking confession. (I think?) I guess he got a lot of good leads. ** When the buses came from San Francisco, it was always about 9 pm on Fridays. We got to know the drivers and they would honk as they approached. We would jump up from the bridge game, and get behind the desk, bar or the tables . . . ready for action. A couple of weeks before they started honking to let us know they were arriving, we would waste time "in place" waiting for them to come. We got in a lot of bridge when they started honking. ** Interesting people came during the week in the winter season. Jackie Jensen (Boston Red Sox) and wife Zoe Ann Olsen (Olympic Skier) came in a lot. One lady from Carson City came in, had a drink and asked if she could play blackjack. Claude said he would deal to her. They spent a couple of hours and she lost around $5,000. Nice day at the track!

One day Tiger Novak told me to go down to the bookie and bet $20 on a boxer who was fighting on TV on the Pabst Blue Ribbon *fights* of the week. I sent a bellboy down to do it. Why I don't know, but did find out later. When the Pabst Blue Ribbon theme song came on TV that night, Tiger climbed out of the Casino Cage and sat in a captain's chair in the lounge. In the first round of the preliminary fight one boxer got hit big. Tiger didn't wait for the count. He got up and went back to work. When I asked him how he knew, he said that there is a difference between gambling and investing! So much for boxing on a national level. **One day a man and his daughter came in the hotel. They were from Bakersfield. I had no idea where Bakersfield was. I learned later! She played the harp well, and was very pretty.

We negotiated a deal where she would play in the lounge and we would give her a nil rate on a room (our worst rate and room) for six weeks. Marjorie Trammel attracted some attention, and was a very nice young girl. She even helped around the hotel. After six weeks I signed for her residence so she could get a divorce. I never asked details. Later when we lived in Las Vegas, we saw her on stage with Fred Waring and his Pennsylvanians. I guess they weren't *all* Pennsylvanians. Years later when we moved to Bakersfield we met and talked to her parents quite often. They said she was happily married and lived in the East and still played the harp on occasion. Strange world!

Cathie learned to deal blackjack in the winter; I learned to bartend. We had to join the bartenders union for $25. There were minimal dues, and when we all took a leave . . . they warned us that the $200 life insurance benefit wouldn't apply. We guessed that was OK! ** We got a state report that the pool water was bad (we sent in samples every week.) We checked with Pete The Pool Boy and he said that he took the water from our tap. I forget how we handled it, but were pissed at Pete for not doing his job. Then again, maybe he helped us.

In the winter we had a couple of brothers who worked for room, board and $10 a week. We paid them in quarters and they took about one hour to get them back into the slot machines. ** We had a crazy cook who lived across the street at the Sierra Lodge. When he left he would leave with his chef's hat on, and we wondered why until we found that he was smuggling steaks out under the hat.

When we first got there, they connected the switchboard. Cathie had the first try. Someone called and she didn't know where to plug them in. She answered another call which was the same. She just plugged them in to each other, and 30 minutes later they came down the stairs together. They asked to see the manager, and Cathie said he was not here. They then asked if the owner was here. She said "yes." They asked to speak to the owner and she told them they were speaking to the owner. They laughed and went out to dinner or whatever.

Friends and relatives did stop by on occasion. They got taken care of well and appreciated it. We would get away by sneaking off to some of the few other places for dinner . . . and to the South Shore for shows. Tahoe was catching on and preparing for the Olympics.

Back in New York City . . . for a short time . . . We had subleased our apartment at 165 E. 35th Street. When we got back to NYC we settled in. Sadly we got there close to Election Day, so we decided to vote. That cost us NY State income tax, although not much because we didn't have much income! I worked selling time at RVH, and did OK. It's forever when the stations pay you, and you're not on a salary. I might well have had a draw of some kind. I did have a small expense account. It was different from the West, and we both missed the West.

Jackie Gaughan called me and asked if I would like to be advertising manager for the Flamingo. He owned 10% and had some say. I told Cathie about the offer and she said "Hell Yes!" We told our parents about it, and none were happy. Much later my Dad told me that Frank Tindle had called him and asked how he felt and what they should do. Dad said he told Frank that there wasn't much they could do, and that we might learn. The Tindles had discussed with their widower friend about buying "Ducket Beanbag Ashtray Company." Looking back I wonder how that would have tanked. Dad had said he could get me in at Stearns & Foster for a few more years. Anyway we decided to go. In December 1958 we headed from NYC to Las Vegas. A great experience followed. Jackie Gaughan met us at the Flamingo Hotel and showed us around. Claude Favarot from the Biltmore had befriended us, and he knew of an apartment on Rexford Drive that was for rent. It belonged to Ken Swanson, the guy who piped the audio race and sports results to all the joints. At that time there were only about 16 apartments in *all* of Las Vegas. The Vegas columnist Ralph Pearl had a bit about Ed Hopple being the new Ad guy at the Flamingo. We were going into our apartment adjacent to theirs when Jan came out to introduce herself. She then called Gordon at the station and told him who lived next door. Small world. The beginning of a lasting friendship . . . and one of the "Y's" in my road. Las Vegas details to follow!

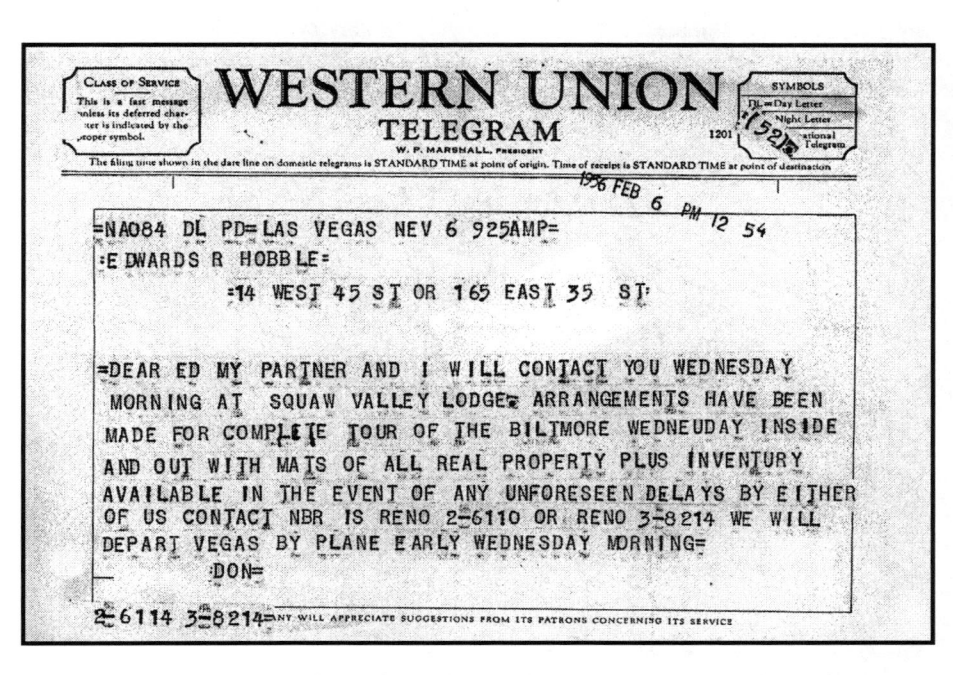

The telegram regarding the Tahoe Biltmore . . . changed our lives.

Vance, Knowles, Rokeach, Hopple and Dobson learning at a crap table.

The Cable Car bus in March 1957.

From the Biltmore parking lot . . . in later years.

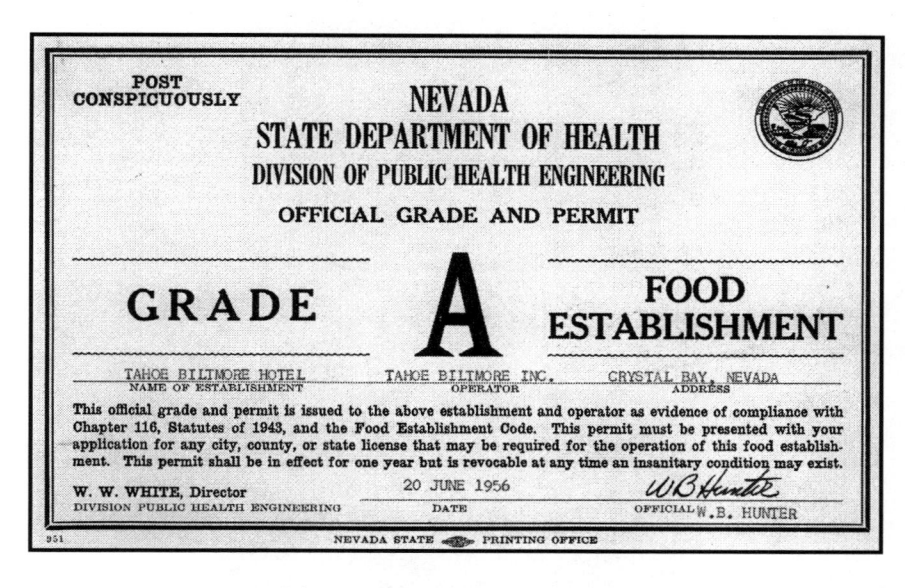

Health Department permit in 1956.

Lounge around the Copper-hooded fireplace in the spacious lobby.

The copper fireplace on the second floor of the Biltmore.

Hopple, Dobson and George Mason at the hotel.

The help and visitors at the pool during our reign.

Dave Crow and Tom Abdo at Dave's house . . . after we left.

Chapter 4 . . . PERMANENT MOVE WEST

In The Las Vegas Era . . . December '58 to September '61 . . . Cathie and I settled down in our little apartment adjacent to the Sherwooods. They were nice to us, and a couple of weeks after we arrived they invited us over to meet some friends. Among them were Bill and Norma Grant who worked for Western Airlines; Father Talley and Lillian Jarrett (he was the assistant, then head priest for the Episcopal Church in Las Vegas); The Jim Costellos who had the Lucky Lager Beer distributorship (they also had other beers and wines). Talley Jarrett went out of his way to say that he wasn't Roman . . . and invited us to church. The Grants and Sherwoods went to church there. It was a new church building, and very nice. Talley and Lillian became great friends. That gang had a lot of good times together.

Meanwhile, back at the Flamingo . . . it was a good job . . . slightly high profile. I worked the national and local print ads (with an ad agency in Los Angeles). I did local ads, radio, newspaper, weekly booklets, TV etc. You never knew how well you were doing. My job included taking the postal cards that patrons had filled out on the dinner tables. We mailed them free . . . but I scanned them all in case there was something wrong that might be corrected. Most were great comments on the hotel and the show. Maybe patrons thought someone was going to read them besides the addressee. ** The Ad agency prepared the postal cards . . . 4 x 6 inches. The talent really watched their billing on the cards, ads, the marquee, the columns, and elsewhere. I had one act that had second billing. It was contracted to be 50% of the headliner. This dance act argued that their billing was only 48% of the headliner. We had to redo all 5,000 cards and correct that. Very picky! I met many celebrities, and some were very nice and others were very hard to work with. Big players would like their pictures, with the headliner(s). When I called some of the touchy acts, they would say they couldn't make it. Soon I learned to call and ask if 2 pm or 4 pm was better for them. They would pick one . . . we would meet by the pool (where the Flamingo sign was prominent on the diving board). The Las Vegas News Service would take the picture (they were very good). They would deliver one to me and send one to their local newspaper. That's how Las Vegas became a household word.

I had the power of the pencil, and that was convenient. We would comp all the News Bureau people, other "flack" artists at the other hotels, and media people etc. The other hotels would do the same for me. At that time there were no "produced" shows. All the lounges and showrooms had acts. That included the Strip and downtown. Vegas was the only place in the world where you could get three eggs for 99 cents or 99 bucks.

The Flamingo also had a yacht on Lake Mead. A number of times I was obligated (ha!) to take someone on the boat. We had the kitchen pack a lunch . . . fabulous . . . and we went out fishing, or seeing Hoover Dam, or some such. One time I had Ted Williams of baseball fame. Our chief host, Abe Schiller, came with us. Abe always dressed "Western" and did ride in the Rose Bowl Parade many times. ** One time they overlapped a day in the lounge contracts with Harry James and Count Basie. The place was packed with only a small ad in the Las Vegas Sun, saying both bands would play one night in the Lounge. The music was outstanding. I guess they were playing for each other!

The job was interesting, fun, but also tiring. Many evenings they would wake me up at 11 pm and tell me to come out to the Lounge. On one occasion they said that Marie McDonald was marrying Harry Karl and they were having a party in the Lounge after the second show. I'd have to get up, put on a suit and tie, call the News Bureau, and get out there. Stars from all the shows on the Strip started to arrive about 1:15 am. The likes of Jack Benny, Groucho Marx, Nat King Cole with Dinah Shore, and many more came. They asked where they were supposed to sit, and the Lounge host and I would aim them. I'd get home about 3:30 am and have to get back to the "Flam" by 8:30 am. Exciting but tiring!

One time they called and said that Elizabeth Taylor was coming to the midnight show. Eddie Fisher was at the Desert Inn, and she probably sneaked out to see Burl Ives and Company. They had just finished "Cat On A Hot

Tin Roof." I saved Kings Row and Queens Row . . . sort of 5th row center booths. She was very nice and took one of the booths. She had a couple of people with her. I signed the comp, and as they left she thanked me very nicely. ** Often times there would be national columnists, and I would set them at our show (or another). Acts like Pearl Bailey would acknowledge them from the stage . . . this impressed them.

All in all it was a great adventure with the nice Flamingo people and the rest of the media and casino flacks. I finally got worn out and Sherwood asked if I would like to come and join the KENO gang. His partner on location (there were 5 owners, mostly in Seattle) Fred Von Hofen had gone back to Seattle to run a station for a high profile station group, and Gordon needed someone to work with him at KENO while he sold time and did promotions. Fred remained a good friend of Gordon and Jan, but he just couldn't handle the Vegas atmosphere.

About the Atmosphere of Las Vegas in the late 50's . . . During our time there weren't many production shows. The first was the Lido at the Stardust. There were a number of them long after we had left Nevada. On the Strip there were a dozen resort hotels and each had a showroom and a lounge with entertainment (the talent was top notch at all the places). ** Reno had more people, but Las Vegas was growing . . . and now outshadows Reno by plenty. Nevada still has only one US Congressman and two Senators . . . so it isn't very populous. ** There were two newspapers, and each had a number of columnists who covered the hotels and entertainment.

People knew each other . . . and the rounders (casino workers, bartenders, waitresses etc.) stuck together. The non-rounders had an affinity, and we knew the clothing store owners, insurance men, doctors, lawyers, judges, and other professionals. They were a neat group, and included some hundred Ph.Ds. who worked at the Nevada Test Site or Nellis Air Force Base. I'm sure the Mafia ran the town, and there was no trouble. We entertained at home or went to fabulous restaurants, of which there were many. It was a good life, fun people, and good times. As it grew after we left, that atmosphere disappeared . . . Corporate ownership took the charm out of almost everything. I guess there is always change. We loved it with lots of space, grass, low buildings, and small-town living in a high profile venue.

My Time at KENO Radio . . . The Seattle Group had come to buy the station after Gordon and Fred had come to broadcast the boat races on Lake Mead. They worked from the ABC outlet in Vegas. They saw it was suffering . . . made a deal . . . and bought the station from Maxwell Kelch. ** The owners from Seattle included Gordon's father, Capt. Sherwood, Jan's father, Les Craigen (a pharmacist), Howard Anderson (ad guy in Seattle), Ed McLaughlin (a CPA), plus Gordon and Fred. They were congenial, and came down once in a while for fun. When Gordon told them that he had talked me into joining the team . . . they obviously wanted to meet me. Ed McLaughlin, the CPA partner, was doing the station books in Seattle. Things weren't going too well. He suggested that we get a local CPA. Vic Fisher had an announcement of his practice in the Vegas newspaper, so they called and interviewed him. Vic was from New Jersey, and had moved to Las Vegas to establish a practice. He caddied at the Desert Inn while he was getting his license. They all thought he was the man because he was older, looked and acted very professional, and had an old briefcase and glasses. They figured he would be a perfect person to keep a thumb on Sherwood and Hopple. He took us as a client, and the Seattle gang went back home. Little did they know that Vic was funny, had a system on the horses, was a par golfer, and liked the ladies. He did keep us straight and we got to know and like him very much. (When we went to Bakersfield and Seattle, he did our work.) A great association!

In short we built the station up in the ratings. We got to know the advertising community (which was growing). We did crazy things and got good ink on it. We set the world's record for broadcasting live from an operating taxi cab. It was when the Rat Pack was at the Sands, and the dispatcher would get personalities and celebrities in the cab. All riders got a card saying they rode in the cab breaking the record for live broadcasting in a taxi cab. Don Hinson, one of our incoming DJ's, did the stint . . . and he learned plenty about the people and geography of Las Vegas. We did the same with the Navy's help to set the record for broadcasting live under water in a swimming pool (maybe it was a small lake).

We also had celebrity guest DJ's. We built a snowman in the middle of summer. ** We had the KENO Parade of Homes, The KENO Talking House, The KENO Kissing Kar, and Kathy Keno . . . the in-store demonstrator. **Our DJ's took a month to build an imaginary boat in the studio and people would come down to see it. ** The announcers were crazy, but good, and so were the promotions. ** We went backstage when Sinatra and the Rat Pack were filming and playing at the Sands. They were fun to work with, and we wish we still had the original tapes. At that time the casinos had "star" entertainment, not production shows. I can't remember how many we recorded for the Sand's commercials.

KENO eventually became #1 in the market among 7 or 8 whistles. Among the personalities were Bob Salter, Jerry Dexter, Laure Vitto, Dan Gates, Dennis Havens, Don Hinson and others ** One day a man showed up at the station from U. S. Playing Cards Company. He pulled out one of *our* calling cards. Trudy, our secretary and den mother took him into Gordon's office. I wondered what was going on. **We had printed some calling cards with the "bee" deck on the back. He said that it was copyrighted and that we had to quit, although he thought it was a great idea. He did ask how many cards we had, and Gordon said about 2,000. He said it was OK to use them but *no* more. We agreed and he left happy. We only had about 300 so we called and ordered 1700 more. I don't think it made any difference in the realm of things!

When Gordon got sick, Jan wrote Frank Sinatra a letter saying that he should buy the station. His accountant, Mr. Sam Burke, got the letter and stopped by the station to talk. Frank wasn't interested but Danny Kaye had a station or two and he wondered how the combination of our "so-called" talent and Danny's money might work. Sam arranged a meeting in LA with Kaye. Kenyon Brown, the owner of KSON in San Diego was there, and he wanted to sell. In the two minutes we talked to Danny himself, he seemed very nice and told Burke to go ahead. We made a deal . . . a handshake . . . and went home happy. Kenyon Brown died two weeks later. Back to square one! Many of our DJ's went on to bigger markets. We finally sold the station for the highest price ever paid for a radio station in Nevada. There were only 19 stations in Nevada, and FM hadn't arrived yet. Gordon and I got what we thought was enough to buy KMAP-AM in Bakersfield. We did and it worked out well over the years.

Living in Las Vegas . . . it was fun and we were the right age! We met people at church, used the Sahara Hotel for a bank (in case we hit a big ticket or some such). Sherwood had the ability to turn off the business switch at 5 pm and not think about how tough it was. That was an art I didn't have. He would cook, or we would trade out food. I think Sherwood still has some of Luigi's pans. We were both void of resources . . . so I would go to the Dunes

Hotel where we had a $300 a month room, food, and beverage tradeout. I would check in, go to the room, order a bottle each of gin, vodka, and bourbon. Then I'd go home, and come back the next morning and check out. The tab would be $70 or $80 . . . but we had 3 bottles of booze in my suitcase at no cost. ** While I was at the Flamingo, we had only one car, so Gordon traded me out an old Ford. It was transportation to go to work, and Cathie had wheels. ** We helped build the Episcopal Church on Maryland Parkway. We attended because of Talley Jarrett. Father Tinker was the main priest and he was a piece of work. The senior warden had to go out on the Strip and rescue him more than once. He came to our apartment one Friday and said that the Bishop was coming down from Reno to confirm a group (Jan Sherwood was one). He had 49 and wanted 50 . . . So he asked me if I would consider being confirmed on Sunday. I told him I didn't know much about it. His reply was that it was like OCS . . . I'd learn! I did it and have been going to church ever since.

Cathie played duplicate bridge at the Dula Center, and amassed about 100 plus master points. Her partner went on to become a life master, but Cathie had some kids to raise and finally quit "duplicate." She was a very good party bridge player throughout her adult life.

When Doctor Hardy called and said he had an infant girl, we were thrilled. Lori was our pride and joy. We decided we should get a house, rather than live in an apartment. We looked around and they were building a few new houses across from our apartment. We went over and found the contractor (Mel Moss) in the house. We asked the price, and he said about $27,000. When we asked what we had to do to get it, he said he would save it for us and took our name and address. In Western style, his word was his bond and he *did* save it for us . . . 545 E. St. Louis.

Our parents insisted that we should put a deposit down, but we told them it wasn't necessary. One day after work we went over to see what was new in the house and Louis Prima was in there talking to Mel. Mel said that he had promised it to us. Louis offered $1000 cash to back out, but we said "no."

It was home for a couple of years. We built a swimming pool. We built a fence. We furnished it nicely, and we had a real home. There was lots of room for a Christmas tree . . . and a couple of dogs. Tidy and Peppy . . . both poodles. We had dinner parties with our friends, like George and June

Mason from Tahoe, the Sherwoods, Bob and Joyce Duffy (and family), Vic Fischer, Tom and Ann Lynch, KENO personnel, and visitors from the East. **Both of our Dads had come to visit us, and they were really delighted to see us and the grandkid(s). I remember when we decided to move West, they were both against it? They changed their minds!

The Sherwoods had adopted two girls, and had moved to a house a few miles away. We visited them often. Howie Kalmensen ran Hank Greenspun's CBS Channel 8, and we hung around with him a lot. (He went on to do radio, built a group called LOTUS . . . and it bought our stations in Bakersfield in 1999 . . . or maybe 2000).

I used to kid about Forrest Duke . . . the entertainment columnist for the Review Journal. We were at Sherwood's one night. Jan asked me to open the door, and it was Forrest Duke. She had told him about my kidding about Forrest Duke, and he said he would come.

We always got invited to openings of the dining room shows. Often the PR guy would call the station and say they had only 100 reservations for an opening, so he said to bring everyone you can find. The "tip" hurt us a little, but the food was great. When the show was over, we would give a standing ovation. A day or two later the national Entertainment Daily would laud the show that opened to a standing ovation. That's showbiz!

Cathie and I were invited to a Christmas party at the only (at that time) movie theater in Las Vegas. It was a good show and great food and drinks . . . a *nice* party! As we were leaving Dr. Hardy came up to us and asked if he looked like Santa Claus. In a way he did. He said he had a Caesarian coming up on December 23rd. Were we interested? Cathie said "yes" if you'll keep "it" until after Christmas. He agreed, and that's how we got Meri. Cathie had taken very good care of Lori, so the Doc had confidence in us. Both of them had an official adoption in court. The gavel was dropped by Judge George Marshall . . . who was a friend of ours as far back as Lake Tahoe. He even kept our dogs when we took a few days off.

We took a short vacation . . . now and then. We went to Buffalo to see Cathie's parents; we got to Underwood to see my parents; we went to Scottsdale on a tradeout at Jokake Inn. It was great, and when we went again they put us in some fabulous accommodations. I think the manager liked us. We also went to Seattle to visit Gordon's folks, and got to Death Valley where the hotel was great. When not on vacation, we worked *hard!* All in all we were there at a terrific time. The mob ran the places. There was no trouble. The schools and hospitals were very good. The people were friendly. It was nice . . . maybe too nice.

Everyone you ever met and his or her relatives ended up in Vegas. They would invite us to a show. We finally got to the point where we would meet them for a drink between shows, which was plenty. If they did want reservations, we could do that easily. They appreciated it.

I joined the Chamber of Commerce 20-30 Club, and when we went to conventions . . . all the casinos would give us a case of whisky and some silver dollars. We would send the money to a bank in that town, and then fake a holdup to get the cash. It always made headlines. We always wore Western clothes, and every morning the big guru would give us 10 silver dollars and a fifth of booze. I was young enough for it then.

The last year we were in Las Vegas, we built a new studio and office on Paradise and Flamingo roads. The guy who sold the property to us (7+ acres) had a piece next to it that was a triangle with a couple of hundred feet on Paradise Road and worked back to a point. There were power and/ or telephone lines on it. I remember it because they wanted $1500 total, nothing down, and $50 a month. I didn't have the dough, so I passed. Today there is a filling station on the Paradise Road side paying $5-6 grand a *month*. Story of my life! The new building was great . . . but the moving was horrible. We had to get out of the old building before the new one was finished. We operated from a trailer on the new property. When the building was complete, it was nice. Maybe that's what helped sell it to the Max Hurst and the Revlon people. Jack Stoll was the media broker, and he told us about a station in Bakersfield, California. People said it was a neat place, so we went down to take a look. Gordon, Bob, and I decided to buy KMAP, a good music station in Bakersfield . . . going broke. The Seattle investors liked the money, and Gordon and I got what we thought was enough to make the Bakersfield station work! NOT!

It was easy to sell our houses in Las Vegas because it was catching on, and real estate was going crazy. We finished the station sale, took good care of our people there, decided to take a month off . . . and we did. The DJ's Dan Gates, Don Hinson, and Dennis Havens wanted to go to Bakersfield with us . . . and they did. Duffy, Sherwood, and I were off and running (we thought).

The Time between "Good Bye Las Vegas" and "Hello Bakersfield" . . .
Before we took off, the Duffy's, Sherwoods, and Hopples drove to Bakersfield. We each bought a house. The Duffy's hung around Las Vegas and then went directly to Bakersfield. Gordon and Jan went to Seattle and the Hopples went East. We spent about 4 weeks around Buffalo, the Canadian shore, Underwood, and Cincinnati. In Buffalo Meri (2 years old) was spitting up all the time. The Tindles insisted that we have her checked by their doctor in Buffalo. After three days they came to the conclusion that she would quit when she started standing up and spitting on herself. They were right! Jan Tindle was worried that it would stain the carpet. Frank said not to worry. He'd get her new carpet if it was necessary. He was a great guy!

Meanwhile in Vegas, Duffy and Gates were watching our stuff get packed and shipped. We had bought a three-bedroom house at 2706 Driller Avenue and our stuff was in it when we got to Bakersfield. The Duffy's also had a house at 2513 Blade Avenue, only a few blocks away from our house. (Joyce still lives at 2513.) It was nice to have responsible people do the hard work for you! We all were situated in *our* new station, and were ready to roll. We knew we would miss Las Vegas a little, but it *did* wear off. It was the best decision we ever made. The details of life in Bakersfield follow . . . my last "Y" in the road.

About The Chairman:

Jackie Gaughan has been a resident of Las Vegas for more than 40 years. During this time, he has become one of the city's foremost citizens, building a spectacular career in the gaming industry. With his expertise in civic affairs, he has worked diligently to improve the Las Vegas image, and is involved in both civic and social concerns. As a casino owner, his current properties include the Union Plaza, El Cortez, Gold Spike, Hotel Nevada and Western Hotel. He also has major interests in the Las Vegas Club, Showboat Las Vegas and Showboat Atlantic City. With a handshake and a warm smile, his hands-on managerial style and inspirational leadership has stimulated employee commitment in providing guests excellent service and satisfaction. In the city known throughout the world for Fun, Gaming and top-flight Entertainment, Jackie Gaughan stands as a landmark of success in the "entertainment capital of the world."

Welcome

Welcome to the Union Plaza Hotel and Casino. Our philosophy here is a simple one, and it has worked successfully for me for over 40 years. First and foremost is our dedication to our guests who want a lot of fun and recreation value for their dollar. You'll get great food, rooms, and entertainment, all at more than reasonable prices. We offer a wide variety of low to high limit table games, and the latest state of the art slot and video games set to produce winners. Innovative contests and promotions combined with winning odds have created a great gaming experience that keeps our guests coming back. Our staff is trained to pay attention to the little things and give our guests the personal attention they deserve, because we truly believe that what makes us better than the rest are our employees and the atmosphere they create. So enjoy your stay, feel the winning attitude, and leave the details to us, but most importantly keep one thing in mind — that gambling should always be fun.

Jackie Gaughan

A later picture of Jackie Gaughan, a "Y" in my road.

A summer promotion at the Flamingo.

The family on a short retreat at Jokake Inn in Scottsdale, Arizona.

Dick Odessky

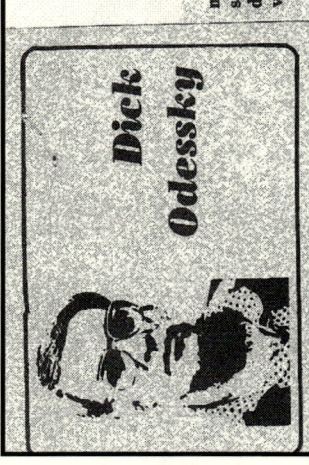

THE GOOD OL' DAYS

WHEN WALTER WINCHELL reported a meeting of hoodlums in the lounge at the Sands and said as the result of the meeting a Florida underworld figure would be killed? Two days later the victim's body was found?

When the Flamingo's "Champagne Tower" was a landmark beacon for traffic coming into town from L.A.?

Then, when the Fremont Hotel was acclaimed as the tallest building in Nevada?

When diminutive Jakie Freidman was president of the Sands and was best known for his spectacular cowboy outfits and his style of shooting craps only using hundred dollar bills?

When C.D. Baker was Mayor; Al Kennedy was Police Chief and Glen Jones was Sheriff?

When Roxie's brothel, located in what's now known as East Las Vegas, burned to the ground one night?

A GREAT BEGINNING

Dollar chuck wagons at El Rancho Vegas

Dearie, do you remember......

When the Sands and the Desert Inn were the two top money making hotels in town?

When every hotel on the Strip served a chuckwagon dinner for a buck. And they included prime rib, fresh lobster and all other sorts of goodies?

When Jake Kozloff introduced the Mary Kaye Trio in the lounge at the Last Frontier, thus kicking off the era of big name lounge entertainment?

The wild parties staged in the El Rancho Vegas showroom by owner Beldon Kattleman? And they never began before two in the morning.

When Roger Foley was D.A. and his deputies included a trio of comers named John Mowbray, John Mendoza and George Dickerson?

When Sheriff's Captains Ralph Lamb and Lloyd Bell were assigned to patrol the growing Strip, which then consisted of seven hotels?

(Continued from page 6)

Odessky remembers

WHEN SAHARA AVE. was San Francisco St. and Tropicana was Bond Rd?

When there was no charge for late shows and the Sahara ran out of beer and Cokes during Eddy Arnold's performance?

When every star appearing in town made the Silver Slipper their final stop of the night, watching Hank Henry and Sparky Kaye in the greatest burlesque show ever and not leaving until after the sun was up?

When Alan Jarlson was entertainment columnist for the Review Journal and this reporter held the same post at the Sun?

WHEN COMEDIAN Lou Costello started dealing blackjack at the Flamingo and wouldn't give up the deck until the house had lost more than ten grand?

When Susan Zanuck and Gregory Ratoff starred in what was acclaimed as the worst show ever in Las Vegas and Beldon Kattleman was stuck with them for two weeks at El Rancho?

When the Desert Spa burned to the ground even before it opened?

When the Royal Nevada closed, the Dunes went broke and the Riviera and Tropicana nearly busted out all within a couple of months of each other?

When the Thunderbird was the haven for the highest rollers in town?

If you remember everything listed here, you have been on the local scene for at least 25 years and probably remember a lot more than we do.

Read Dick Odessky in The Valley Times

Early Las Vegas recollections.

Another vacation at Jokake Inn.

The family at our new house, 545 East Saint Louis in Vegas.

Dog Peppy inside the new house.

Don Hinson overlooking a KENO "Kissing Kar promotion".

Friend Claude Favrot with Lori in our apartment on
Rexford Drive before the new house.

Jan Sherwood and me prior to attending some show opening.

The Diocese of San Joaquin, Protestant Episcopal Church

The Duties of Wardens and Vestrymen

The general function of the Vestry, as the laity's representative, is to represent the best intelligence, most loyal Churchmanship and most earnest piety of the Parish in matters temporal and spiritual:

¶ To forward in all practicable ways the spiritual interests of the Parish, as becometh Christian men holding sacred trusts, and so far as is consistent with the headship of the Rector;

¶ To assist him as far as possible both by means and personal cooperation in his agencies and methods for the maintenance of piety and good works;

¶ To aid in persuading parishioners and others to attend church on Sundays and other occasions of public worship, and to see that all comers are met with a Christian welcome; and

¶ To encourage among the parishioners, by word and example, the principles of Stewardship and concern for Christian Outreach beyond the limits of the parish.

In regard to the property and finances of a Parish, they should exercise a fiduciary relationship, giving to these matters the same concern as they would to their own personal problems of property and finance.

Their trusteeship in temporal matters has a spiritual bearing and should work in and with, and be in subservience to, the great object of parochial organization, the ingathering of souls into the fold of Christ.

Vestryman

Bishop of San Joaquin

Rector

Chapter 5 . . . SETTLING DOWN

Bakersfield . . . the Final "Y" in my road . . . Cathie and I moved there in 1961. I still live there. When we arrived the Duffy's had been there a couple of weeks. They met our moving truck and got everything set in our house at 2706 Driller. It was a real deal for us. Meri and Lori were very young. I had to work hard to try to get KWAC on the road. Cathie took care of the kids . . . found a doctor for the kids (Dr. John Forney), and got to meet the neighbors.

We had the only swimming pool around, so it was a gathering place for kids and adults. We got to know Jack and Bev Hislop and their kids . . . Bill Anderson (East) and their 4 kids . . . Bill Anderson (West) and his son [the Andersons lived next door to each other . . . thus the directions] . . . Eugenia Eyrabide and family. The Duffy's and Sherwoods would also hang around. Later there were others, like the Reynolds et al.

It is only fair to say that I remember a number of incidents, but my time line is really askew. Readers may not remember it as I have . . . and that's OK . . . and they're probably correct time-wise. It makes little difference in the long run . . . so here we go!

While Cathie was home working, I went to the station early. It was in the middle of downtown Bakersfield in the Padre hotel, and was lousy . . . both the station set-up and the hotel. We did two main things. The existing format was Golden Music . . . dying . . . so we changed it to Rock. When we had all the promo's and records and radio stuff together for a format change, we had the announcers read the telephone book for a full 24 hours. That caused much word of mouth and people started listening and wondering what the h—we were doing. Then we started the rock format . . . and with some promotions, it caught on quickly. We moved the operation to 1330 Chester Avenue. It was an old but big building. We acquired news vans and promo items, did remotes and threw dances. It was work but it got us known.

We did skywriting around town. We found someone who would change the seat signs at the Bakersfield College football game . . . So when the fans waved the cards . . . instead of saying "Drillers go . . . (or some such) . . . It said K W A C—1490. That was a coup! We had changed the call letters . . . asking for a number of them associated with humor. We ended up with KWAC . . . for K-whacky. The doctor who had an announcement of his practice in a newspaper ad right above ours didn't like the "quack" association. I guess he got over it.

We wrote a series of four letters prior to changing the format, and sent them a couple of days apart . . . to 150 prospective advertisers. They were hand written by our wives. They tossed some perfume on them before mailing. They had innuendos like "your touch thrills me", "enjoy my sister on the Coast", "I'll give you my number tomorrow", "I'll see you this Friday". All were signed R.K. This woke up a lot of people. Most thought it clever and couldn't wait for the next letter. Some wives who worked in the office raised hell with their spouses. The Police Department had stakeouts on a number of mail boxes . . . but the wives mailed them by chance in different mail boxes every time. When the last letter arrived it said *Radio KWAC* . . . gave our frequency 1490, the address, and phone number. That day the Chief of Detectives came to our office and asked what we were doing. We told him it was just a promotion, not a shakedown, and showed him the series. He told us we had caused a lot of consternation among citizens . . . and the Police Department. We apologized for any trouble. He said "OK" . . . and as he left he winked and said it was one hell of a promotion!

Our news was 5-minute KWAC-a-matic News on the hour. We had billboards to promote it. All the billboards had a light on them, and the board read that if the light was flashing, KWAC-a-matic NEWS was on! We had lots of comments . . . and got sponsors!

We had dances in many venues, and had high profile groups. We had the BEACH BOYS one night for $200. Their father cashed the check, and gave seven of our DJ's $20 each. [that's payola].

The old station had the BAKERSFIELD SINGERS on Sunday morning. It was a black Gospel Group . . . and they were very nice. They owed the old station some money (our purchase included the Accounts Receivable). They worked hard to get sponsors, so I told them that if they could finish paying the old bill . . . I'd let them ride for free. That worked until we sold the stations. They appreciated it. The advertising sales helped them pay for their building. I feel good about that.

Ed York, a promoter, had the Bakersfield Speedway. He worked us over, but I got to like him. I invested in the speedway . . . and surely gave them lots of advertising. But alas . . . didn't make any money. While KWAC had the rock format, we brought in the Glenn Miller band under the direction of Ray McKinley. Both York and I sat in $500 seats . . . again no money. We brought the Shrine Circus to the Auditorium. I think we broke even but I learned plenty about circus promotions and operation. Fascinating!

We also promoted Midget Car Races in the new Civic Auditorium. That was fun, but the Auditorium made us discontinue because of the fumes. Ed also had Advance Ticket Sales at the auditorium, but they soon took that franchise away and did ticket sales in-house. (As an aside, Ed moved to Fresno and South Carolina . . . doing carpet cleaning . . . Running the association and becoming the Man of the Century in the carpet cleaning business. He retired in Vancouver, Washington in poor health, and passed away in 2006.)

Other than work . . . We had neat neighbors, and would congregate at our pool on weekends. Sometimes we had to work at dances or remotes, so time with the family was precious.

Joyce Duffy heard of a baby for adoption, and mentioned it to us. We followed through, and the lawyer (Roland Woodruff) came to see us. He said that the one we had heard about wasn't available, but he had another one. Making a long story short, we adopted infant Susan. ** Doctor Forney liked Cathie, and we saw him socially off and on. She could always get an appointment or phone call with him. At 2 years Meri swallowed lye in a neighbor's back yard, and Dr. Forney was right on the case. He enlisted Dr. Cunningham and Dr. Sheldon . . . and they saved her life. At 4 years she was in the hospital more than she was out. Meri got a lot of attention in the hospital. She knew everybody. Cathie and I went every day, and when Lori had a bladder infection, she was most willing to go to Mercy to find out what was going on. When Meri got out, Cathie started volunteering at Mercy and did so for the rest of her life. After a number of operations, and dialations . . . Meri went on to live a normal childhood. She still has the girl's 50-yard breaststroke record at Bakersfield High, swimming that is!

Going it alone at the Radio Station . . . We had an opportunity to acquire a construction permit from the FCC for an AM station in Kirkland, Washington (Seattle). When it was approved, we gave Dexter Hammond a check for about $7,000. He went to the bank that afternoon and asked for a cashier's check. Everett Murray was the manager, and without blinking he gave them the cashier's check. We had about $500 in the Bank of America. Everett called and told me what he had done . . . and suggested we get some additional capital. I told him that if we did, it wouldn't be ours. We covered it in a day or so . . . not sure how. Jan Sherwood and I had discontinued "kiting" checks with our Seattle and Cincinnati banks . . . at their request.

Jan and Gordon moved to Seattle to build and run the new acquisition—KYAC. We had helped a building permit owner in Phoenix start and build a station, which we programmed in a black format. It went well. We decided to make the Seattle station format black. That left me alone in Bakersfield to run KWAC.

We were encouraged to turn the format to Spanish Language. We did that, and hired all the early morning Spanish language personalities . . . like Esteban Lopez Sierra, Carlos Zapian and Marie Elena Anderson . . . who was the Spanish Voice of Bakersfield. If you asked the Chamber of Commerce something about Spanish, they would quote Maria Elena. The format was Spanish until 2 pm, then black programming until 7 pm, and Country & Western in the night. It was crazy to have three formats, but we wanted to keep our English language sponsors on the air. Soon the Spanish caught on result-wise, and we went ALL Spanish Language . . . 24 hours a day. We had permission to go 1000 watts days, and 250 watts nights. It was pioneering with lots of interesting after effects.

The station became so strong that Cesar Chavez filed a Petition to Deny our license with the FCC. It took us 10 years to get out of it . . . so we were tainted and couldn't apply for another station anywhere. We wanted an FM in Bakersfield, and I had Hal Brown tied to a contract for KIFM (the first FM in Bakersfield). He had taken $5,000 as a down payment on a $50,000 sale price. It would have been a GREAT property.

We didn't get the $5,000 or the FM station . . . and the situation probably ultimately cost us a couple of million. So it goes. The idea of a Petition to Deny is that you should talk to the complainer and settle your differences. He would never meet. Cesar just said that the FCC would decide. That left us in limbo for years. He wanted the station. People said that I should give it to him, 'cause he's going to get it anyway. I said the hell with him. He didn't get it !

Adding Stations to our group . . . Things got tough for Gordon running KYAC in Kirkland. With a black format, a strong black personality talked a bank into loaning him the money to buy KYAC . . . a token loan I guess. The sale went through and Gordon and I got some $700 a month for a couple of years. Gordon retired and did some work with audio in Albertson's stores in Washington. KWAC in the meantime leased and then bought KCHJ in Delano. It was and still is Spanish Language. We also applied for an FM, after Chavez was eliminated . . . he got nothing! We got it because at that time we could buy out other bidders.

When we built it we decided to program it with CLASSICAL music. The reason was that all the other stations in town would recommend us when asked about Spanish. We didn't want that to quit, so we picked a format that wasn't in town. Bob Duffy did most of the work, and the town loved it . . . it got the highest ratings of any Classical station in the country.

Advertisers didn't savor it so much. We did promotions, and really pushed it . . . but alas, the schools loved it, the service clubs loved it, the country clubs loved it . . . but the advertisers *did not* !

Finally we saw that Spanish was going into FM strong, so we changed that KIWI format to Modern Spanish. It really took off. Classical might average $27G's a month billing; when it went to Spanish it would exceed $100G's a month, and it only stole about $10G's a month from our other stations. We were on a roll! In the meantime, KMAP, Inc. (the Corporation name wasn't changed, although the radio station call letters were) was sending Sherwood money every month. By the May before the stations were sold at the end of 1999, Gordon had gotten mucho dollars in the mail from KMAP, Inc.

Spanish Language was catching on. Chavez's union had a station operating from Bakersfield but licensed to Taft. Nobody would report them for fear of retribution. They also had a *non*-commercial station north of Fresno that sold time flagrantly. Again nobody wanted to report them. They had clout with Ted Kennedy et al.

Spanish TV came in the market, and other operators decided to get a piece of the pie. Our manager, Mike Allen, said he thought it was time to sell. Howard Kalmensen, whom we knew in Las Vegas, had developed the LOTUS GROUP. They sold a station in Chicago to Disney, and needed a 1031 exchange of assets deal. It worked for both of us. We sold all three.

We had given some employees some KMAP stock. We bought Gordon and the employees out, and now Mike Allen and I have all the stock in KMAP. We did have a little play with 1050 AM and Disney Radio, but radio was getting tough and we weren't that interested. Mike and I sold to Sacred Heart Radio, a group of Roman Catholic radio stations, and it is doing religious programming.

That is the story of Bakersfield Radio from my vantage point. Radio was very good to me. I had a good time . . . met some great people . . . had loyal clients . . . got good results . . . and wouldn't trade a day of it.

Now about the Social Side, the Community Service Side, and the Extra Curricular Side of Bakersfield . . . there was plenty! I don't know where to start!

The family lived on Driller Avenue until June, 1969. We moved to 2131 Elm Street in June, 1969, and lived there until 1994. In January 1994 we moved to 2300-58 El Portal Dr., in Tamarack Pines. It was really sizing down.

During the "Driller Ave." era . . . we met a number of friends from throughout Bakersfield. **The three girls took swimming and diving lessons. They became very good at both. **At the radio station we traded out lots of "stuff" and spread it around to friends and neighbors. Our pool was the meeting place for the neighbors and their kids. We had birthday parties and trips to Swensens ice cream shop . . . in our new Chevy convertible . . . or the old limo we acquired somewhere . . . or on our bicycles. **Somehow I bought a horse . . . PRINCE . . . whom we boarded at Ace's Stable. Paula Anderson loved to tend to him, and brought him up to Driller Avenue once in a while. The kids would all take a ride, and loved it.

I got hooked on trying to ride a unicycle. As I tried day after day, the neighbors would sit on their front porches, laugh, and watch me try. Believe it or not, I did finally learn to ride it and everyone was amazed. There are movies of it for proof.

Ken and Dottie Ramsey became our lifelong friends on a tradeout trip to Las Vegas. That's when Dottie got the name "Dirty Dottie". We met at an Ad Club meeting. They had two sons, Mark and John, and daughter Jennifer was still in the pot. We got to know Judge Jack and Doris Lund and their three daughters, Leslie, Julie, and Tracy while skiing at June Lake and then later in church at St. Luke's Episcopal. We got to know Don and Gwen Brown from Rotary, IHOP, and Bill Wright's Steakhouse on Union Avenue. Pat and Sid Sheffield became our good friends, as he was assistant to the President at Cal State Bakersfield and was in my North Bakersfield Rotary Club. Pat was a dedicated teacher.

Through many years, these four couples met every Friday for cocktails at one of our houses. We then went to dinner, the cocktail host choosing the location. People called us the "Four Seasons." The parameters stated that the restaurant had to have wine . . . at least . . . and meals for $10 or less. It worked. This started in the "Driller" era, cleared the lengthy "Elm Street Era" and into the "Tamarack Pines" era.

The gals went to Rosalie Stubs dance studio . . . which had a recital at Harvey Hall. It was June '65, and the title was "Beautiful Kern." I remember Susan was a Cuddly Duck, Lori was a rainbow, and Meri tapped . . . as the Sherwoods and Hopples watched from the side. You could see Rosalie behind the curtain, dancing the routines and cheering them on. It was a riot.

There were swimming meets and diving contests at the park. Most of the kids on our street participated . . . and did well. ** I bought a Jamboree motor home/camper from Larry Radanovich We took it to June Lake. We would ski and then the kids could do their homework on our way back. It had a "john" which everyone appreciated and used! We also took it to Park City and *Williams Ranch*, and others took it various places. The truth is that we wore it out!

The Ramseys would go to Carpenteria in the summer and stay at the Sands Motel . . . on the beach. We did the same, and so did Denny Ralston and family. We had some great times there . . . playing tennis with Denny was a kick. He could sit on a stool and beat Ken and me so easily it was sinful. ** The Ramseys and I decided to build the biggest Banana Split ever. We used a turkey roasting pan . . . cut over thirty bananas, and added a gallon each of chocolate, vanilla, and strawberry ice cream. We invited all the kids in the complex . . . maybe 20 . . . to come and bring a spoon. Some parents came too . . . and partook! The kids dumped cans of chocolate sauce, caramel/butterscotch, and strawberry gook on it. Kids loved pitching the cherries on it after the whipped cream. We even added nuts. It was a neat affair and I'm sure the kids remember it. The next year we did an ice cream soda in a big plastic waste basket. It was memorable too!

One morning I was at Lorene's Coffee Shop on 24th street for breakfast. Jerry Pence, a real estate man, was there. Somehow I said that I was looking for a new house that I could entertain 25 or 30 people in the back yard. He said he had one that 100 people would be lost in. I told Cathie and she said we ought to look at it. I told Jerry that Joe Salas was my real estate guy. Jerry said he could have the commission, but didn't need to do anything . . . (When we bought, Joe credited us with his commission). When we went to see it, Cathie said that if we ever got that house . . . we would decorate the big pine tree. Somehow we closed the deal, trading our Driller Avenue house as a down payment. That was the beginning of the "Elm Street" era.

We loved Driller and the friends on the street . . . we stay in touch with those that are around today. None live on Driller any more! While there, neighbor Jack Hislop got us into Stockdale Country Club . . . the dues were $33 a month. I still belong, and the Stockdale monthly dues are 15 times that much! ** Bev Hislop sponsored Cathie in Junior League. She met some interesting people, but really was not very hot on it. It was an honor *then* . . . and she treated it that way.

I got a real estate license . . . how I don't know. Jack Low at the station wanted some help/advice, so I said I would help him. The only way I knew how to help was to take the test and then help him get set for the repeat. You could do it every two weeks in Sacramento. We flew up on a trade, cramming all the way. Somehow I passed that time. I must have had a flat 70%. I helped him and he passed it the next time. I still have a real estate sales license, but I'm not sure why.

Cathie and I joined a number of associations and non-profit groups. They might be detailed elsewhere in this book, if I get to it.

The "Elm Street Era" . . . was 25 years and really great. 2131 Elm was a neat big house . . . over 5,000 sq. ft. It was built by A. H. Karpe in the late thirties, and then sold to Dr. Fenderson. He sold it to us. When we owned it, it was referred to as the "Karpe" house. When we sold it in 1994 to the Thompsons, it was referred to as the "Hopple" house . . . or the "Christmas House".

It didn't need anything when we moved in. It had a fenced pool, and a not-quite-legal tennis court that was good for volleyball. It had basketball hoops at both ends, and fruit and nut trees around. It opened onto an alley in the back . . . where we had orange, lemon, lime, apple, peach, pomegranate, and grapefruit trees. Quite an orchard, except that people kept hijacking the ripe fruit. We still had plenty left.

The girls each had a room and bath of their own. It had a family room with a projection booth; there was a study with a fireplace which I used as an office. The formal living room was big and the fireplace with a marble mantel really set it off. The formal dining room had a buzzer to call the help, but we didn't have any. It had an alcove in the dining room that we could put a Christmas tree in . . . and we did. The kitchen had a pantry, bathroom, laundry section and some 43 cabinets and/or drawers . . . plus a laundry chute from a bedroom on the second floor.

The girls grew up in that house . . . went to Cardin School and then Bakersfield High. They would bring kids home to swim or play volleyball. Many liked it because we had two slot machines in the family room . . . it was easy to get baby sitters!

It was really a party house and yard. We had a number of weddings in the back yard. Lori and Mark were married in 1988 and had their reception in the back yard. It really looked nice. (We had a conversation and decided that he really wanted to be a doctor. I said I would help, and I did. He spent ten years studying, but he made it. It's a terrific success story, and we're all so proud of him.) We also had other wedding receptions, anniversaries, birthday parties, and yearly station Christmas parties. Many charities and/ or service organizations often used the back yard . . . such as St. Luke's and other churches, Mercy Hospital, Rotary clubs, Ad Club, Cancer Society, etc. Thru the years it was a busy backyard! A lot had to do with the fact that the we always allowed people to wander through the house . . . use the restrooms etc. Many famous backyard party venues didn't allow that.

On our first Christmas in the house, Meri had told us that the shower in her bath didn't work well. We decided to get her a new one. I called Trent Jones and he said he would put one in on her birthday, December 23rd. That worked for us. I was called at the station and told that they couldn't turn the water off . . . They had called California Water Service and they couldn't either! It turns out Mr. Karpe had a meter hooked to about half the locations, and had put a line *directly* into the water company's main line for the remainder of the locations. CWS put a meter on that and it cost me about $900 a year more than I had been told the water bill would be. That's over $20G's the 25 years we lived there.

We did decorate the big pine tree in the front of the house, as Cathie had mentioned when we first saw it. I traded out 25 sets of outdoor lights with Nello Foxx. We had been told about someone at CSB (now CSUB) who did the trimming. I called him and he said he would trim the tree. We figured out that when he was at the top . . . he could throw a rope down, I could tie a string of lights on it, and it would light the tree. We had some big star or Santa which we put on the top. When we lit it about December 15th, the phone rang off the hook and people started coming down the street.

Our gardener (Florencio Jacinto) thought that we should trim the other big pine, so the second year we did. We made a *BIG* peppermint candy cane that looked like it was sticking thru the dining room alcove roof . . . and replaced the Christmas tree with a *Huge* stuffed bear who was licking the cane that went through the roof in the dining room. We added lights on the front hedge.

I was building a "Rubics Cube" looking toy box for one of the kids for Christmas. It was 2x2x2 ft . . . each side a different color . . . and electrician's tape to make it look like a Rubics Cube. Someone said we should put it on the roof and illuminate it with a flood light. I thought the roof came to a point, but found out there was a big flat roof up there. (As an aside, the gals would sun bathe up there in the skinny . . . only the Sheriff's helicopter could see them . . . and came by often)! I put the Cube on a stand and put it on the roof and put a flood light on it. BIG MISTAKE! Word got out that the biggest Rubics Cube anywhere was on our roof. Word spread at schools, I guess, because we started having traffic jams in front of the house . . . TV stations would cover it . . . The Californian covered it . . . and the "Christmas House" was on its way.

Every year we developed a theme . . . Olympics, Statue of Liberty, Disney, Energy Saving, all kinds of "in vogue" word and computer games. At first we did it all ourselves . . . with volunteers. The Fords, McCarthy's, Lunds, Sheffields, Browns, Ramseys and others at times helped plug in lights, decorate the inside of the house, and set the roof decorations. The team got rather good at it. The Browns brought hot dogs and served lunch . . . I took everyone to the Pyrenees for dinner the decoration night. **In the last couple of years, the decorating excitement for our kids had worn off . . . so we had some artists do the picture stuff. We still installed.

At its peak, the Auto Club would send a towtruck to the area for a couple of hours because every night they would get calls about a disabled car in that area. The line was always three blocks long, because when they got to the house cars would slow up to take a *good* look. One night I got into the line and then drove into the driveway. Another car followed me, and said he thought it was a good idea. I said something like . . . but I *live* here.

As years went by more neighbors would decorate, and it was a very festive area. Since then a number of other "areas" have sprung up, but I think Elm Street was the first, excluding Panorama Drive that used to have the Christmas Parade floats parked in their yards. **A few people would come by and ask to play Santa Claus . . . and we said OK. We always had some candy canes for a Santa to give out, 'cause we didn't want him to just say "Hi . . . Merry Christmas" . . . etc.

The house always was serenaded by groups. We would give them
Christmas Candy . . . and sometimes a donation. People would write
us and thank us for providing the Christmas Spirit. **The post office
would forward us mail addressed to Santa Claus . . . a chapter out of
Miracle On 34th Street.

Happenings during the Elm Street Era . . . During this time (1969-1994)
so many things happened. The kids grew up; we took a bunch of trips; we
made many friends and helped many causes; we bought *Williams Ranch*
in Pioche, Nevada; we sold it too; our Underwood camp was purchased,
Las Misiones condo(s) were purchased, Kids were married; grandchildren
came along; I took lots of vacation time, and the radio stations worked
better without me around; Cathie and Jerry Hoos ran the Candy Stripers
at Mercy and Cathie really enjoyed working in "admitting" at the hospital.
I'm sure I have forgotten the funny and fun things that occurred. What
little I remember I won't forget! My best recollections follow in no particular
chronological or order of importance.

At 2131 Elm we had great neighbors. Andy and Pat Anderson lived next
door, and they invited some of their friends one Saturday to their house
for food, booze, and to meet us, their new neighbors. Among them were
Margaret and Bill Moore (he was President of Tejon Ranch, and they ended
up living "cattycorner" from us), George and Dodo Nickel; Jim and Bebe
Burke; John and Barbara Forney, the guy we rented the Radio Station
building on Chester Avenue from (KWAC probably owed him rent, but
he didn't say anything), Dorothy and Dusty Jamieson . . . (he was a lawyer
and great piano player), and Fred and Rebba Green. There may have been
others. Fred Green always looked like he came out of Esquire . . . never
without a tie.

Somehow in the conversation Mattoon, Illinois, came up. Cathie and
I didn't have too much to say in this high profile group, but when he
mentioned Mattoon, I said that in Mattoon, when you dial "desk" you
get the owner of the telephone company, and "Mary" you get his wife.
Fred asked how I knew that. I said that I had gone around with Peggy
Lumpkin. He said that Peggy's mother was *his* sister. The group took
notice . . . my stock went way up . . . and now I was somewhat of a
socialite instead of a radio peddler. Jim Burke said to come see him at
his Ford dealership, etc.

We ate and played bridge, and they were impressed with the way we (mostly Cathie) played.

George Nickel asked me about what I thought of the property he offered to the college (CSB) out in the Rio Bravo area becoming a tennis complex. I told him I'd ask Ken Ramsey, who was a good friend of Denny Ralston. At 7:00 Monday morning my home phone rang and it was George Nickel. He reminded me that I was going to arrange a meeting with Denny and Ken. I did same that day and we all agreed to meet at George's office on Stockdale Highway that week. That meeting started the Rio Bravo Tennis Ranch. It was built, started running and was the beginning of the Tennis Club, the Lodge, the Rio Bravo Golf Complex, and that area. Cal State Bakersfield should have gone there . . . it would have been *beautiful*! Ken and Dottie Ramsey worked there for a while. I was a director and it's first President. Andre, retired or stolen from Bakersfield Country Club, was the first chef. It was a hidden gem for some time, but somehow the Nickels decided to sell the place. It's there today, but I don't know much about it. I guess my friends and I are getting too old.

I was always giving away trade-out stuff, and was generous in other ways . . . so Cathie decided she would do something for me. She got Darrell Van Wyke to get one of the last of the VW Beetle convertibles . . . 1978 was the year. She says that in two days Darrell had come up with one, and she only had half the money. She called Frank Toller at California Republics Bank and said she needed $3000 quietly to pay for the car. When she went to the bank the next day, the check was waiting. She said she signed something with her name misspelled and she left.

One night when I came home the gang was there, and they coaxed me into opening the garage door. There was the VW . . . with a poster board sign saying this was FIVE years of Christmas, Valentine's Day, Easter, Anniversary, Birthday, etc. I still have that sign in my office. It was a real surprise . . . and useful when one of our cars was in the shop for something or other. After 30 years it only has 10,000 miles on it, and lives on Susan's property in Cayucos. It looks good!

In 1973 I won the AAF Silver Medal. It was awarded at a local Advertising Club meeting. Ken Ramsey was President that year and that probably had something to do with it. It was an honor, the silver medal is really nice, and I still look at it once in a while with fond memories of the advertising community in Bakersfield.

For a project for the Kern County Bi-Centennial, the Ad Club decided to re-publish an old Bakersfield book called "Shotguns On Sunday." Don Hopkins of the Better Business Bureau found a printer who would do it, and got the original author, Joseph Doctor, to OK it. It was about the rough gambling, bars, and "murderers" that ran the town in its early years. Many people remembered it, and bought copies. It was a good addition to the Bi-Centennial events.

At the Bank of America, my banker, Everett Murray, was a neat guy and he liked me. He is the person who got me into the Santa Barbara Clinic, where I have had my annual physical for many years. It was there that they found my prostate cancer . . . treated it early . . . and I'm still in remission. Anyway, Everett and a couple of locals like Frank Sill and Bud Reed started working on an infrared machine called the "Hot Spotter." It could see heat in transformers . . . and the TV screen gave it a reference. With this you could fly along power lines and picture the transformers and film it. Then electric companies could repair the "hot" ones. We used it at some factories etc. but the fact was that the electric companies had their own system of maintenance, and the older guys running it didn't want change. It was interesting, but we finally sold the patent and sample machine to someone. I don't know who, but they probably made some bucks and use it today.

I joined North Bakersfield Rotary in 1967. I worked as the Bulletin Editor . . . then the Secretary for a couple of years, and then in 1978 I was President. It was a good year. I was known as "Silver Dollar Ed", because at the weekly meeting I would flip a silver dollar to a member who had done something worthwhile. Both Cathie and I are/were Paul Harris Fellowship members. Our Club met at the Veteran's Hall on Roberts Lane in Oildale for a long time. We then moved around to places like the Holiday Inn Select, and are currently meeting at the Petroleum Club. I still go when I'm in town, but my classification is Senior Active . . . so I don't have to make up missed meetings.

In the middle seventies the Bakersfield Californian got colored printing presses. Judy Clausen called me and asked if they could take my family's picture in our back yard for the Father's Day paper. I said "yes" . . . they did . . . and it was the *first* front page colored picture in the Californian.

I saw an ad in the New Yorker about the First National Whistle Off being held in Carson City, Nevada. It sounded interesting, so we took the Jamboree and drove up for the occasion. The Ramseys, Sheffields, and Lunds went with us. I nosed around the venue (it was the lawn of the building where the Legislature meets) and found the ad guy for Adam Computers, the sponsor of the event. I asked who the judges were, and he asked if I wanted to judge. I said I had a real judge with me, and he said they would let him judge too. He gave me a couple of *big* badges with "judge" ribbons. Back at the Casino Jack and I wore the badges. Participants asked if we could be bribed. We told them that we could, and that we drank scotch and bourbon. We never bought a drink after that, and we didn't know who they were. The great DJ Jazzbo Collins was a judge too. We did the best we could . . . had a wonderful time . . . met some very interesting people . . . and went home Sunday quite satisfied. Later the participants were asked to critique the function. They stated that it needed better judges. They were right. The next year we went with the same gang plus John and Shirley Uhran. We saw much more, but didn't judge! A great weekend!

Somehow I was appointed to the Cal State College Advisory Board. It was a sounding board for the President to ask about how certain decisions would be accepted in the community. I was President of it for a year. Then College President Jack Frankel called me and asked about someone he was thinking about appointing to the Foundation Board. It happens that I am truthful and told him what I thought. He then asked me what I thought about putting him on the Advisory Board and moving me to the Foundation Board. I told him I questioned his judgment, but I would like it. He appointed me to the Cal State (now University) Foundation. It was a big step up! A dozen of Bakersfield's high profile people . . . and Ed Hopple. I blended in . . . did my stint as President . . . and am now a Life Member of the Foundation. Amazing enough, I have a vote at a meeting . . . but I'm out of the loop and don't go. I do support it, though.

Our dog Peppy was a miniature poodle. He had a birthday coming, so we decided to throw him a party. We invited all our friends' dogs . . . and told them to bring their owners. We had no idea what the hell might happen.

Ten dogs with 20+ owners came to our house one Friday night. The dogs were dressed to the 9's . . . some wore ties (cut off below the knot). Jane Toller made a round birthday cake of dog food with mashed potato frosting and colored decorations. I think she used pretzels for candles. It looked *SO* neat! The balloon lady showed up with her dog. She entertained the dogs. We drank and the dogs behaved so well, it's hard to believe. Even Peppy "knew" it was his affair, and acted extremely well. No one could believe that there were no accidents, fights, etc. among about ten dogs that didn't know each other! God was good.

When KIWI was classical music, we had a trip to England to watch John Farrer, the Bakersfield Symphony conductor, record a CD with the London Philharmonic Orchestra . . . maybe the Royal Philharmonic Orchestra. Anyway, they recorded in old churches around London. You pay to do this, and I helped John with the bankroll. You rehearse (play) for four three-hour sessions. You may use 20 minutes of each session for a CD. We watched him do it twice . . . even my friend Bob Vance came over to watch. Those CD's and many others are still around and available. John has been a great friend ever since. Now we give the Symphony their office on 34th Street, so I see him regularly. He and Bonnie moved into the Anderson house next to our 2131 Elm just after we left. I gave him my big "Elm Street Playboy Club" neon sign, but now he isn't sure where it is. He has since moved, and Jim and Robin Scott moved in with their talented kids Jack and Riley.

The return to *Underwood* and buying a camp in 1985 was during this time. Our purchase of condos in *Las Misiones* San Jose Del Cabo, Baja Sur, occurred about 1991. I'm still there! Lengthy details of these and other events follow later. We have to get on our way to Tamarack Pines!

Selling 2131 Elm Street . . . Kids had gone to college, or gotten married. Cathie and I were spending 4-5 months in Cabo and 3 months at Underwood. The nest was empty. We had no thought of selling the place, when Mary Christianson knocked on our door. She said she had someone interested in buying the house. She said what they were willing to pay, and I said that I wasn't interested. I told her that if someone from out of town came in to run one of the big companies and "his" wife wanted an older house with amenities in town, I might be interested. She said that the potential buyers were going to buy something down on the river and build if they couldn't make a deal. *

After she left, I told Cathie what she had said. Cathie asked why we don't sell it . . . we're never here, and it costs plenty to keep it even when we're gone. I asked her . . . "Where would we live?" She said Ralph and Ruth Cunningham had a neat place. We called Ruth and Ralph and asked if there was anything for sale there. They said there was, and we should come out for a drink and look around. We did, and saw #58 at 2300 El Portal was for sale. We talked to them and made a deal. ** I called Mary Christianson and told her that her people could buy Elm Street with a good offer. The only caveat was that they had to decorate for Christmas. I left all the decorations, lights, etc. They accepted and we started packing.

It is neat to have both the old and new house for two weeks . . . which we did. That made moving easy. Cathie threw things away while I wasn't looking. The joke was that the bag ladies were coming down the alley in limousines to get the "pitched stuff". We were obviously sizing way down. We got it all taken care of, threw a "house cooling party", and moved into Tamarack Pines. The kids have fond memories of 2131 . . . so do the grandkids. It was a wonderful house to grow up in . . . party in . . . play in . . . and just plain live in. We were so lucky to have had the opportunity to experience it.

About Tamarack Pine at 2300 El Portal Drive . . . The Cunninghams had steered us right! Our new home, #58, didn't need anything done to it . . . save getting rid of some fluffy curtains, etc. The complex is walled and gated. All the buildings are duplexes with one common wall. The condo with our common wall was owned by Eloy Renfro, whom I had done business with for over 20 years. He was a neat guy.

Cathie got to know some people in the complex . . . and everyone seemed very nice. There was/is a recreation room, swimming pool, hot tub, and all the amenities . . . including barbeque grills, guest parking, and strict rules. There is a common mail box section as you come in the gate. I enlisted Jeff Olson, who lives in #63, to pick up my mail and put in the mail slot I installed in our garage door. It has worked nicely for over a dozen years, and Jeff has gotten some pocket money.

Four times I came home from the office to the wrong address . . . ol' 2131 Elm. I finally got out of that rut. It is much closer to Stockdale Country Club than our other houses, but we didn't go there much more. Many of our friends threw a surprise "house warming" party in our back yard. Marilyn Curtis catered it, and it was neat. Between Cabo and Underwood, we weren't there too often, but it was secure and all we had to do was shut the door, turn off the answering machine, cancel the paper, and take off. That was a real break from 2131 Elm where we had to have someone house sit.

Early in the game I decided to convert the top of the garage to an office, which I did. It is a neat place and has a fire pole to the garage. As an exit, it lowered my insurance.

Eloy Renfro was going to sell the adjacent condo, and I bought it. I think Lori lived in it at some time, but we then acquired 1921 Glenbarr Court, where Lori and Mark lived while he did his internship at Kern General. They went to Illinois for his residency in anesthesiology at Rush and lived in Villa Park. Glenbarr is only about eight blocks away from 2300 El Portal.

Meanwhile Susan was in college at Long Beach, and then transferred to Barrington College in Warren, Rhode Island. She was in the last graduating class before it combined with Gordon College in Massachusetts. At this writing granddaughter Abby goes there.

Meri went to college at Chico State; she worked, and then got married. They lived on Manning Street (about 12 blocks away), then somewhere else near by, and finally into the house at 1921 Glenbarr Ct.

Meanwhile Cathie and I took *trips and cruises*; she volunteered at Mercy Hospital while I worked at the stations. We had acquired three or four condos at *Las Misiones* in Cabo San Jose, Baja Sur and all our friends visited us when we were there in early January until early May.

In 1999 we sold the radio stations to Lotus Communications. Howard Kalmensen had developed that group. He was a friend of ours in Las Vegas, and was the one who convinced us to change the format of KWAC to all Spanish language. KMAP (the corporation) acquired the 1050 AM frequency and ran Disney Radio for a couple of years. We didn't do much with it, and we treated it like a stepchild. We finally sold it, and we were out of the radio business.

In the Spanish station sale, we acquired a set of buildings known as the Kern Foundry on 34th Street. Mel Atkinson found it for us and still manages it for us. I have an office to go to there. I do when I'm home. ** Cathie's mother, step father, and father had passed away during our Bakersfield stay. My sister Sal also died . . . too soon. ** My Dad and Janet moved into an assisted living place in Cincinnati . . . Dupree Terrace. It was a great spot. Janet was failing, and she passed away in December 1999. I went to see Dad every month until he passed away in December, 2004 . . . at the age of 102+.

The Love of my life, Cathie, was failing but wouldn't tell. She was going to CBCC for radiation and/or chemo. She went by herself, didn't want anyone to help her, and kept up a wonderful front. She wanted to go to Megan Gallagher's wedding in Denver, and we went. I think she flew by herself from Bakersfield and I met her in Denver. I was coming from Cincinnati on one of my monthly trips. She enjoyed the wedding, and we came home on Monday.

She died the following Sunday, June 10, 2001. Meri and I took her to the hospital on Friday night. Coincidentally, Susan was in town for something . . . and Lori and family had arranged a Bakersfield vacation for that week, coming from Illinois.

Many friends showed up at the hospital. Dr. Mark helped us all. Sister Barbara and Mal Clinger chartered a plane from Jackson Hole, Wyoming, and got there just before she passed away. I don't want to dwell on it because it was so quick and it hurts . . . but Barb and Mal helped me pick out a plot at Union Cemetery. She wanted a tombstone, didn't want people to walk on her, and Union Cemetery was the only one that allowed it. Although we went to St. Luke's, we had the funeral at St. Paul's Episcopal downtown. It was loaded . . . and Father Wilcox and Father Mark Lawrence presided. He later became the Bishop of South Carolina.

Cathie had said that we should keep the Stockdale Country Club membership in case we needed it, so I called and they were full. We had the celebration of Cathie's life at the Bakersfield Country Club after the private services at Union Cemetery. Friends came from all over the country. Friends housed some, and the Sheraton had a field day. I *know* she would have approved of the church service, the burial, and the celebration of her life . . . and it's fair to say she was pretty particular.

I had been diagnosed with prostate cancer metastasized in 1993. I was in remission, and still am . . . but Cathie and I often talked about one of us going. We *both* agreed that the other should go on living life to the fullest. At that time we figured I would be the one to go first. NOT! I miss her but I have gone on.

I went to Underwood alone the summer of 2001. Everyone was very nice to me. I got home in September and was wondering what I would do next. I guess it was laundry! I went to Cabo for the November meeting and stayed about three weeks. When I got home I tried to get things in order. I went to New York for the annual Economic Bordello Christmas Lunch. The whole family spent that Christmas in Cabo. It was fun but we all missed Cathie.

In mid December I was coming back from the pool at Tamarack and I saw Kae Babcock doing some paperwork on her patio. I said "hi", and she asked if I wanted a glass of iced tea. It sounded good so I went in the patio gate. It turns out that she was doing Symphony Associates invitations . . . and I was interested because we give the Bakersfield Symphony their office in our building on 34th Street.

When Cathie and I had returned from Cabo in April 2001, Kae was in her front yard doing some gardening. She asked where we had been this time. Cathie told her that we had been in Cabo, and asked when *she* was going to come down. Kae asked which month was best, and Cathie told her that February was very nice in Cabo and not too good in Bakersfield. Kae said she would come down next year on the eighth of February. Cathie said "great!"

Meanwhile, when I was sipping the iced tea on her patio, Kae said that she assumed all plans were *off.* I told her I was honoring all contracts and she was welcome. The topic of the Symphony Ball came to light, and she asked me if I would like to join her table . . . there were going to be about 10 friends. I thought about it and said that I might do that. It was late in January, so I said that we could both fly to Cabo a few days after that. **Somehow she softly implied that she would like me to wear a tux. I went to Cathie's grave and asked her if it was OK to wear a tux to the Symphony Ball as a guest of Kae Babcock . . . a neighbor that Cathie had known pretty well. I heard Cathie say . . . "for Christ sake, why not?"

The "Ball" was very formal and very nice, and I had a good time. It was at Stockdale, so I could buy a few drinks etc. The people said that Kae and I looked very good together. After the function we made plans to go to Cabo, and we did.

I introduced her to the Las Misiones family, and they liked her very much. She stayed a long time because she liked it and we got to know each other. We both seemed happier. I invited her to Underwood that summer and everyone there liked her. ** We began going places and doing interesting things. At this writing we are still doing same! *Neither* of us thought that we would ever find happiness with another, but we both found out we could love again. Ain't love great!

People thought that my condo at Tamarack Pine needed some sprucing up, so I contacted Janice Parker . . . the wife of an old buddy Dave Parker . . . about doing something to upgrade #58. It turns out she had done some of the original decorating, so I hired her and told her to use her own judgment . . . . Kae and I were leaving for Underwood the latter part of June and wouldn't be back until September. She said she would finish it by then, and she did! She did a good job!.

I rented the adjacent condo to Cheri Zimmerman . . . supposedly temporarily . . . but she has stayed there all this time. She married Gary Banducci. He helped put up the Christmas lights, and she watched the place when I was gone. In November 2007 they bought the condo from me, but she still watches out for my interests when I'm gone. She has been a wonderful neighbor. I really appreciate that!

In the last few years we got to know Terry Hill (of Oildale Winery fame) and Sheri McKieghan who lived in the condo behind Kae. They are fun but they are moving north when their condo sells. We'll miss them and their dogs.

Details of events, places, and stuff I remember are chronicled in this book somewhere. Kae and I still live in Tamarack Pine, spend Novembers and winters in Las Misiones in Cabo, and our summers at Underwood in upstate New York. We veer off the routine once in a while, and in January 2009 Kae and I are going around the world on the Queen Mary 2 . . . 85 days. We're "S K I ing" . . . that's Spending Kids' Inheritance.

LIMITED PRODUCTION

"2131" BRAND

ESTABLISHED 1969

GROWN, CARED FOR, PREPARED AND PROCESSED WITH GENTLE HANDS AND CRAZY METHODS FOR YOUR PLEASURE BY THE HOPPLE GANG.

2131 ELM STREET

BAKERSFIELD, CALIFORNIA, U.S.A.

NO GUARANTEE OF ANYTHING WHAT-SO-EVER

Label we used on stuff we grew at 2131 Elm.

Recognition well-deserved

When Ed and Cathie Hopple's 2-year-old daughter, Meri, became critically ill, she literally lived at Mercy Hospital for more than a year. Cathie vowed to volunteer for Mercy for their loving care to Meri. She did that and much more.

The next 35 years encompassed devotion to the auxiliary in various offices, including president — but her favorite was the junior program. She and Jerry Hoos guided the juniors for more than 20 years, swelling their ranks to 75 with a waiting list of 100. In the early 1980s, Mercy's junior program was highlighted at California Hospital Association's annual convention. It was a "model program".

Credits abound. Ed and Cathie contributed generously to Mercy as early Friends of Mercy Members, restructuring ER and establishing the information center in the SW. Plaques attest to this.

It is the compassionate side of Cathie not all knew. It was not unusual for Cathie to assist stranded travelers she encountered at the information desk, visit homebound volunteers, bringing teas from Alaska to a Mercy housekeeper. Rummage sales and events at the Elm Street home are legend.

To me, her 35-years recognition epitomizes the two framed sentences that hung in Speaker of the House Tip O'Neil's office for 10 years: "It's nice to be important — It's more important to be nice".

RUTH N. LOMBARD
Bakersfield

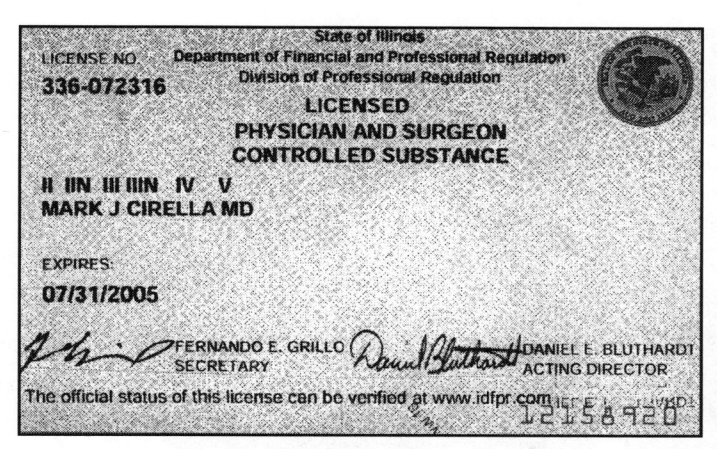

Dr. Mark's 1st license.

KWAC's first station building on Chester Avenue . . . with fleet.

First Bakersfield home on Driller Avenue.

Janet and Dad's summer home in Michigan.

Skywriting to kick off KWAC Radio.

We will serve no swine before its time!

Janet, Cathie, me, sister Sal and Dad in Cincinnati on Dad's 90th. (10/20/92)

The best Business Conference in the world!

About the Home

This lovely French Country home was built in approximately 1938 by Arthur H. Karpe. Mr. Karpe was a Kern County pioneer in farming and livestock. He was a farm implement dealer and sold International Harvester products. International Harvester honored Mr. Karpe by celebrating his retirement from the implement field in his 30-year connection with the company.

The house in the 30's

Mr. Karpe with his prized Hereford.

Mr. Karpe celebrated world-wide notoriety by having bought the most expensive Hereford bull for $65,000 in 1949 at a Pulaski, Tennessee auction. Two weeks previous, the livestock spotlight focused on Mr. Karpe as he purchased the most expensive Hereford female at a Madera auction for $21,000. The newsclippings stated, "he has the greatest stock foundation possible". After his retirement, he devoted his time to his model Greenfield Hereford Ranch and a financing enterprise in downtown Bakersfield.

Mrs. Karpe

Later in the life of this home, it would be owned by doctors and media moguls. Famous stories about fabulous parties and floating boats in the pool are legendary around Bakersfield. The Christmas decorations continue today by our present owners and are enjoyed by the community each year. No "Christmas Light Cruise" in December is complete without dropping by the "house on Elm Street".

A later item about 2131 Elm Street . . . I guess I was the media mogul and did the Christmas party and house decorations.

Daughter Susan at the National tri-athlon (Sept. 1995).

Cathie and Dad in the backyard at 2131.

In Washington DC with my Congressman Bob Mathias . . . Olympian.

In 1956, John Nichols' Vision increased to include a radio ministry. The Lord used Mr. Edwards Hopple, owner of KWAC Radio Station, to make it possible for the Association (to broadcast five-and-a-half hours of air-time every Sunday for 35 years) to bring you the "Spiritual Devotion and Old Ship of Zion" broadcast. The radio ministry has touched many lives with the Gospel.

After 28 years of dedicated and faithful service, on July 13, 1978, John saw another vision -- the place prepared for him, as he went there to be with the Lord.

The Bakersfield Singers—John Nichol's obit.

Partner Gordon Sherwood and Harold Meek at a KWAC Christmas Party . . . Kristy Allen in back.

Me with Bob Kramig and Les Kramig at my 40th Wyoming High School reunion.

A backyard party at 2131 Elm.

Partial backyard at 2131 Elm.

One of the monthly gourment dinners at 2131. . . .
Sid Sheffield, Gwen Brown, Ken Ramsey, Don Brown and
Pat Sheffield. (Feb, 1987).

Here I am at Underwood working on this book.

Underwood club
Of Essex County New York

THE UNDERWOOD CLUB is a large holding of privately owned wooded mountains and springfed lakes in the Heart of the Adirondack Mountains, located about 20 miles south of Monty's Elm Tree Inn. Surrounded by Adirondack State Park, it has housed many generations of families who have relaxed with nature, partaken generously of spirits fermenti, fished, golfed, hunted, bridged, and damn near everything else thru the years. The home of happy memories for many, it is one of the last oases . . . the last of an era where the wet set can "rough it" in luxurious seclusion, or something like that there.

Home made wine label . . . used at Underwood.

Ronnie Purdy at the Elm Tree Inn.

Cutting ice at the Underwood Club.

Bill Ward, Georgie (guide) and me on the
Colorado River one-week white-water trip.

The staff on the private train car trip
from New York to California.

Self Explanatory! Both gave up cigars since,
but not playing gin!

Lunds, Hopples and McCarthys on
JD'S WHITEHAWK in 1992 in the Caribbean.

Stu Real at my 50th birthday party on the
Rotterdam . . . leaving Cuba.

A pet on the golf course in Costa Rica.

Cathie and me on a snowmobile at Underwood.

Tony at ZIPPERS . . . great hang out in San Jose, Baja.

Amateur performance on a cruise thru the Panama Canal. Pro baseball player Jay Johnstone is behind his new wife Mary Jane.

The Christmas House at 2131 Elm Street.

Chapter 6 . . . P.S. . . .

This book wouldn't be complete without a few details from the adventure of the Round The World Cruise on the Queen Mary 2 . . . January 13 thru April 8, 2009. From the Penthouse #9067 here's what I think happened.

Mike and Kristy Allen took us to Los Angeles and we flew to Ft. Lauderdale . . . somehow we got upgraded to business class and it was great. We got picked up at the Miami Airport by Cunard and they took us to the Hyatt in Ft. Lauderdale, Florida. We stayed that night and the next night. We went to a computer store and bought a printer so we could print stuff on the ship. On the 13th they had a gang of people going on the QM2. We put our luggage out, they took it and then transported us to the ship. The lines were a little long, but I had a cane and they let me sit. The Grill guests had a special line . . . they checked our passports, tickets, and visas. We were issued an identification card . . . like gold! They escorted us to our room, which was very nice. It had a big balcony, dining room table, utility bar, desk, TV stuff, 2 bathrooms, a big closet and a big bed. I'm glad we upgraded.

Our dinner companions were British . . . Mike and Elaine Merridew and Bruce and Marian Franklin. They were delightful. Mike is a stock broker and Bruce is retired. They had all been around! On ship they took dance lessons and caught most of the lectures. We missed many because we thought we had plenty of time . . . wrong! We were sorry to see them go in Los Angeles, but we'll keep in touch. Mike and Kristy Allen met us for 3 hours in San Pedro. They brought stuff from Bakersfield that we had e-mailed that we could use . . . and we sent back stuff with them that we were sure we didn't need. I picked up some cash at the Bank of America and we did Ross for Less and Nordstrom's Rack. We bought some doodads, stopped at Starbucks and came back to the ship. That night we met our new dinner companions . . . Ian Hunter and Judy Hall . . . and Robyn and Kingsley Mundey. They were all characters in their own right . . . and we enjoyed them immensely. They are Australians and lots of fun. Judy knew plenty about food. She had been a caterer in New Orleans, but lived in Australia for some 20 plus years. Ian and Judy had an olive oil "farm . . . plantation . . . orchard . . . whatever" and the pictures of it were beautiful. Kingsley is a man of the world, and has a number of businesses. He was interesting, funny, and had some great lines. About managers he said that if they can make money they can do as they want. If they were losing money they were to do what they're told. He also defined realism as an illusion brought on by the absence of drugs and alcohol. All four of the table folks kept us entertained. They got off in Sydney, and we were also sorry to see them go. We toured in Sydney, and then went to the Convention Center for a cocktail party for the "Around the World" cruisers. It was fantastic in every respect. We estimate that there were about 300 full world cruisers. The ship was full all the time, but people were coming and going on all of the four legs of the adventure.

The next day we found out that the 4 people at the next table were moved to our table. We were the only ones left at Table 51, but we couldn't have been their choice. They were interesting as hell, too. All Americans, Park and Lynne Smith are from Flint, Michigan. They are young, very well educated and polite . . . and good looking too! Dick and Mary Myers are from Florida and Maryland. He was the "Clam King" but sold a portion of the business. The story of how they "clam" was fantastic. He had 23 boats, a marina, and God knows what else. He and Mary are very nice. He is in a scooter, and the help enjoyed playing with it when they brought it to him . . . all very, very nice people. We were lucky again! They are all "Around the World" cruisers . . . they even took the UK to New York segment. They were all in penthouses and had us for cocktails.

We took hours in Tokyo, and when we got to Thailand (Laem Chabang), Kae knew a friend . . . Bruce Gladden. He and Pranee came to show us around the city, and they did. It was wonderful . . . and so were they. We got an insight into the Thai life, and it was most interesting. My printer broke so I threw it away and got another one in Thailand. They took us to lunch around 3 pm at a beachside local place. It was super food. We let Pranee order. They then returned us to the ship.

Along the way we met some interesting staff. Our Cabin boy (Eduardo) and Butler (Lily) have been exceptional. They know what you want before you do. It will be tough to get back to real living. In the Grill room (single seating) the Maitre d'Beniamino Acler has been very attentive. Waiters Vireal, Erdal, Mauraicio, Ivana, and wine steward Anil were great. Vireal and Mauraicio left the ship in Hong Kong. Others left in Dubai. In Hong Kong we added Leonardo and Aerjit. They were also terrific. The service and food is magnificent. The ship is a city. The Casino was even kinder than most.

Singapore was "as expected", and Cochin, India, was interesting, but dirty and the traffic was horrible. We rode a tuk tuk (motorized rickshaw) and that was fun. In Dubai we took a tour and became astonished by the new big buildings . . . the indoor ski jumps . . . and all since about 1980. It is said that half the world's cranes are in Dubai. They seem to try to out do the global Jones's. The QE2 was docked there . . . going to be a hotel and convention center they say. Salalah in Oman was small. Our tour went to town. We saw the Incense Museum and 200 tailor shops . . . bumper to bumper along the streets. The jewelers were fewer but all next to each other. It was desert with mountains in the background. You had to have permission to photograph natives. I don't know what they do if you don't ask. Egypt was next.

We got up at 6 am so we could get to the 7:30 call for the trip to the Pyramids, Sphinx and Cairo. It was a long tour but we did see 9 pyramids, Cairo, the Sphinx and camels and TV dishes galore. We went to bed early because we were tired. The next day we went thru the Suez Canal and into the Mediterranean . . . a neat adventure. We next went to Athens, and it is the latest thing in ancient. If they didn't have history, they wouldn't have much except lots of ferry boats and sea coast . . . and a ton of taxis. We next hit Rome (Civitavecchia) for a few hours . . . having rounded Italy and gone thru the Straits of Messina. It rained but we did have great local pizza. Cannes was next, and it rained there too. We tendered to shore for a short tour of Cannes and Nice . . . and tendered back. Lily brought pizza to the room about 3 pm . . . so we skipped dinner. Therese and Francis Drillien (from Cabo) met us in Barcelona, showed us the town and took us to his fabulous hotel (Le Meridien). The hotel, beach, and the food were magnificent. They brought us back to the ship and it was sad to leave them. We left Barcelona and headed toward Cherbourg, France. It had been substituted for Le Havre. We went thru the Strait of Gibraltar and headed north to Cherbourg. We started thinking about disembarkation in a couple of days. Cherbourg was wonderful . . . took a tour of the Saire valley . . . wonderful farm lands and seacoast towns. I loved France. We got thru customs and immigration and got to the bus to Heathrow. We unloaded our 7 bags and checked them in . . . only cost $280 USD for the luggage. They wanted $10,000 for an upgrade so we passed. The economy section was very comfortable . . . good food and drink . . . and great TV. We arrived in LAX tired, and met Leslie in Mike Allen's Sequoia . . . and she drove us to Bakersfield. We got home about 11pm and went to bed. It was a wonderful trip . . . the adventure of a lifetime . . . we met some great people . . .saw some fabulous countries . . . and got back in one piece. It was 84 days of luxury, and it went by fast! I guess that happens when you're having fun.

Kae in a "Tuc Tuc" with the driver in Cochin, India.

This sneaks up on being the end of this book's so-called Section One . . . I guess Section Two follows if all goes well. For now, cheers and "thirty".

111

Details of the trip around USA and Canada with Mr. Robert Hecht in the summer of 1948 . . . Early in this book I referred to Mr. Hecht. We left Cincinnati and drove to Chicago, just the two of us. Mrs. Hecht (Mialata) met us there at the Blackstone Hotel. She was a charming lady, fine pianist, also Austrian. We got acquainted and developed mutual respect along the way. All the accommodations were first class. Our first stop the next day was Winona, Minnesota, where he stopped at a textile mill (so he could expense the trip, I guess). We weren't there long! We headed for the Badlands of South Dakota, Deadwood and Mount Rushmore, then Yellowstone. We stayed at Old Faithful Inn. We then went to Jenny Lake Lodge in the Grand Teton area.

We played roulette anyplace we could find it. I remember the Cowboy Bar and Wort Hotel in Jackson Hole, Wyoming. They were big "illegal gambling" places, and anyone could play. We then headed north to Billings, Montana (where we found a roulette game). From there we went to Glacier Park and stayed at the Glacier Park Inn. Driving a new '48 Cadillac convertible (with fins) was a real joy, and everyplace we went people stared at it. We stayed a couple of nights in each location, and took tours, private boat rides, and saw the sights everywhere. I was beginning to see what this country was about and loved it. From Glacier Park we crossed over the Canadian border and went to Waterton Lakes National Park in B.C. We then worked our way to Banff, and stayed 4 nights at the Banff Springs Hotel. I was really impressed with the accommodations, the grandeur of the hotel, and the assortment of people. They had a 16-piece orchestra in the main dining room. Elevator girls wore white gloves and neat-looking uniforms. I tried to mingle with them, but it was against hotel rules and they liked their jobs! Somehow I danced with a neat-looking older blonde who said her husband was a musician and songwriter and never learned to dance. Turns out he was Jay Livingston who wrote many songs for movies. He was a nice guy and in our conversation I asked him what he had recently written. He said he had done a tune for Bob Hope called "Buttons and Bows," and it would come out in the fall. During the rest of the trip I told whoever would listen that Bob Hope would do a song called Buttons and Bows in an upcoming movie . . . and to watch out for it . . . I was trying to be on the inside, I guess.

We continued to Lake Louise and stayed two or three days at the famous Chateau Lake Louise. At breakfast I picked up a Readers Digest, and on the back was a picture that was the same magnificent view I was lucky enough to be seeing in person. We toured up to Jasper, did the Columbian Ice Fields, and headed to Vancouver. It was beautiful. From there we went to Seattle, and stayed a few days at the Seattle Athletic Club. We did all kinds of tours everyplace, but Seattle was neat.

All along the way the three of us were getting to know each other, and were very comfortable. Mrs. Hecht taught me a well known German ballad, and I taught her "She's too fat for me!" At one time we were following a car that had a license plate 1066. He asked me what that brought to mind, and I said "the Battle of Hastings." That raised my stock considerably. We left Seattle and went to Crater Lake, Oregon.

We then went up Mount Hood and stayed at Crater Lake Lodge. It was a wonderful lodge, and the views were breathtaking. After a couple of days there, a bear ripped the top of the convertible and stole some cherries. We pinned the top and it was OK! We headed to San Francisco. I had a soft drink at the Top of The Mark . . . the Mark Hopkins Hotel where we were staying. San Francisco had some wonderful restaurants—one tropical in a setting where it rained inside. I thought that was neat. We went into a museum, and went directly to Gainsborough's painting "Blue Boy", and then we left. Mr. Hecht said that was the only thing really worth seeing. We might have been in there 20 minutes . . . tops. Next we drove down US Route 1 to Santa Barbara, where we stayed with Lotte Lehmann. She was a famous German opera soprano and the world's best "Lieder" singer. When we arrived she was trimming some trees and grabbing a few citrus fruits from them. She gave us some. (Later in the trip Mrs. Hecht stayed in Los Angeles to hear Lotte at the Hollywood Bowl.) In Santa Barbara we did the Sunday brunch at the Biltmore Hotel . . . as famous then as it is now. We enjoyed the beach, and went to some jazz places. Lotte died in 1976 at age 88 and there is a neat theater named for her in Santa Barbara. I was really impressed with Santa Barbara!

From Santa Barbara we went to Los Angeles and stopped at Lauritz Melchior's home. Melchior was called The Great Dane. He was the #1 Wagnerian Tenor of his time, and was on the January 22, 1940 cover of Time Magazine. His wife, Maria Kleinchon Melchior, was of German descent and he met her as she parachuted into his orchard in Austria. They arranged for us to go to a party given by Atwater Kent. He invented one of the first TV tubes and was

famous for throwing big parties. The tent was the size of a football field and
fit easily into his back/side yard. A bunch of celebrities and hangers-on were
there. Charlton Heston was very nice. It was a memorable evening. We stayed
at the Biltmore Hotel in Los Angeles. We dined at the best restaurants (like
Romanoff's) and went to the nightclubs (Macambo, Tropicana etc . . . where
we saw celebrities like Ralph Edwards of "This Is Your Life", Robert Mitchum,
Betty Grable and so on. (many years later in Bakersfield Ralph Edwards owned
a radio station and we ordered Biltmore Bourbon from the Biltmore Hotel in
LA . . . it was good and priced right and shipping was free).

Mrs. Hecht left us in Los Angeles to see Lotte at the Hollywood Bowl, and
5 minutes after we said goodbye, Mr. Hecht said we were off to Las Vegas.
I don't think she knew, but she told us to go slowly back to Atlanta . . . so
we had time to spare. We went to Death Valley and saw Scottie's Castle . . .
Maybe stayed there . . . went through the salt flats and finally got to Las
Vegas. The Flamingo was brand new, and we stayed there. Mr. Hecht played
roulette . . . we saw dinner shows and late shows. The midnight buffet (which
started at 11 pm) was fabulous and *free*. I guess later the truck drivers found
out about it, and they finally started charging. We went to the Old Frontier
and saw Martin & Lewis long before they split up. We went downtown to
the Golden Nugget, and saw the shows at the Thunderbird and El Rancho
Vegas. It was the beginning of the Las Vegas reputation as a classy resort
destination. I never got it out of my mind!

Mr. Hecht and I left Vegas and headed for Route 66 . . . glanced at the
Grand Canyon, saw the oil wells of Oklahoma and Texas . . . and ended up
in Little Rock, Arkansas. I forget where we stayed but it was First Class . . .
and they had illegal gambling. We found the roulette wheel, and stayed an
extra day. Time was getting short so we barreled out for Atlanta, Mr. Hecht's
home. We got there and stayed at their beautiful house. Mrs. Hecht flew in
the next day. She begged me to come to Austria some time . . . the Salzburg
Festival. She said to come for a week and she would introduce me to the great
musicians and events. I never took her up on it, and it's probably the one
opportunity in my life that I wish I had taken advantage of. They put me
on a Delta DC-3 in Atlanta headed for Cincinnati. It was my first airplane
ride. That trip and the Hechts changed my life!

We stayed in touch for a few years, but time got away . . . and at my last
call she was very weak. (When I was in the army Mr. Hecht came down to

Southern Pines . . . I came over from Fort Bragg and he was so glad to see me. His health was failing, but not enough not to find an illegal gambling place. He took me there for dinner. (I think Rudy Vallee was entertaining.) That was the last time I saw him.

About Music and the Big Band Era . . . the 40's and 50's were the best years in the music business. I really believe that. I think that is why I took up the tenor saxophone. It was basic in the Big Bands. (In high school my dad had me tested for aptitudes. Someone was trying to get Stearns & Foster to use these tests, so he said to test my son . . . and Smitty, my friend. We took the test and music came out high . . . along with math and BS. I have often thought that is why I ended up in the radio business.) During my music impressionable period it was almost all "*Big Band*." While writing this book I asked Chuck Cecil if he had any kind of a list of the Big Bands. Chuck did the national syndicated radio program . . . The Swingin' Years. (He was married to Edna, my friend Don Brown's sister). He sent me a list of a couple of hundred bands, and most of them I had heard in person or on the radio. (Of interest might be that Ace Brigode, who led the house band at the El Rancho Vegas in Las Vegas was the brother of my fifth grade teacher.)

In high school we saw many of them at the Albee Theater in Cincinnati. Vaughn Monroe played at our Amherst Senior Prom. At the Flamingo we had Big Bands in the Lounge . . . Harry James . . . Count Basie . . . Woody Herman . . . Ray McKinley et al. The other hotels had personality shows (as compared with production shows) and most of the Big Bands of the times were featured. Matty Malneck was the band leader at Cal-Neva in Crystal Bay, Nevada when we were at the Tahoe Biltmore. Anyway, it was the *best* time for music with lyrics and melodies. I'm printing Chuck's List, as he sent it to me, somewhere in the book. That's what I listen to today. If you don't, . . . try it . . . you'll like it . . . no, *love* it!

The Bakersfield Advertising Club . . . The Bakersfield Ad Club was a group of people involved in advertising in Bakersfield. It was a member of the American Advertising Federation, which had a yearly convention. There were also regional conventions. ** The membership came from the media with a few advertising personnel from local companies, i.e. banks, Electric Company, Brock's Department Store, ad agency owners, etc. When I arrived in Bakersfield I was asked to join the local club. (At one time I was President . . . but so was everybody else.) We would meet monthly at a place of business of one of the members. It would be catered. It was fun and educational to see the facilities that members used to fool the world. The meetings were short . . . rumors were thwarted or started . . . and generally it was an update of what was going on in Bakersfield that affected the advertising and public relations environment. There were reports of progress on some outrageous local developments. The best I remember was Bill Foulk's report on the underground balloon system being built between Bakersfield and Tehachapi. His final report indicated that the project had been scrapped for lack of funding (and interest).

Ad Club Conventions . . . and beauteous camp meets they were! The meetings lasted about three days. Spirits fermenti prevailed! Various vendors would have suites and invite people to come and meet their people and toss down one or two. We had well known speakers. Some of the National convention cities I remember include: Dallas, where Jimmy Carter (then President) was the speaker; Chicago had leading advertising agency Presidents . . . very high profile. The Washington DC and New York meetings deserve a paragraph of their own, which will follow.

The regional conventions I remember were Bakersfield, Palm Springs, Portland, San Diego, and Spokane. ** Palm Springs was a funny one. Member Dave Parker had a couple and called the President. He asked them to call back, but they said that the President of the United States does not return calls. Nice screen. They opened a new TV station in Palm Springs, on our hotel property. It went off the air at midnight . . . but the engineers were running some porno "after hours" and didn't realize that the transmitter was on. I suppose they picked up a few listeners.

In Spokane the newspaper threw a big Salmon Bake. The owners didn't drink, so we were warned that if we wanted a spot or two we would have to bring it and leave it in the trunk of the car. We did. They did serve a punch with dry ice in it so that it bubbled. The parking lot had a hundred cars in it and 95 had open trunks. The host was oblivious to it.

The Bakersfield convention was a nice affair. One thank-you note said that Bakersfield had it and we drank it. One leading Seattle ad agency owner brought his family, and his daughter ended up in jail. Member Jack Low had clout and got her out quickly . . . no charge. They were *very* thankful.

We published all the speeches and events and gave everyone a copy. This way they could learn about meetings they didn't attend, and had proof that they had been to the convention. All thought it was a nice touch.

Washington DC American Advertising Federation Convention(s) . . . The conventions were often held in Washington. It was a neat place to do same. The Dow Jones company threw a big cocktail party at each national convention, and the ones in Washington were at the Smithsonian. You would get a drink and then wander away and see some great stuff . . . meander back to get another . . . then repeat same! ** There was a welcome party at the convention hotel, and it was early in the era of the TV show Laugh In. Someone was running around quoting that funny guy's phrase ". . . want a Walnetto?" . . . People were laughing. We decided to find out if we could get some Walnettos. We called a candy distributor. The guy that answered said he had some . . . $5.40 a box. I told him we would give him $20 if he could get a box to the bell boy's desk. He was only three blocks away, and leaving to go home. It was on his way so he said he'd gamble and bring one. I think he was astonished when he got there and delivered the Walnettos, took the $20 and left happy. We started going around the party saying the same line . . . *and* then handing them a package. Soon the word got out that Bakersfield really had them. That was the start of our so-called popularity at conventions.

Jim Evans from a Virginia TV station invited us up to their suite to hear the infamous *Frozen Owl* tape. It was a funny 20-minute tape . . . similar to a roast . . . which they had developed with the help of a couple of shots. Jim became Col. O. W. Long, and all enjoyed the tape. Bakersfield asked for a copy of the tape and he said he would send it . . . and he did. At the following year's convention he said that he had brought the tape. During the year we had had it put on disc . . . 10 inch acetate with a great cover. I remember it said "see other side" . . . which was the same thing. People kept turning them over until they caught on. We gave him 20 or so albums . . . which he loved. The word got out and people started asking where they could buy one. We gave them one! ** Jim Evans (Col. O. W. Long) had a friend leaving the hotel in a limo. As it pulled away he yelled . . . "Write if you get work!" That's where I got the phrase.

At one lunch the waiter had a great uniform. I told him I'd give him $20 for an old one. He said for $20 he'd get me a new one, and he did. I told him my room number, gambled by giving him the $20, and it was on the bed when I got to my room. ** I used it in Bakersfield when Jack Lund and I would wait table for the Chinese dinner that Sid Sheffield gave for charity every year. The dinner had a high profile . . . and so did the waiters.

I learned a little about the national press when we had Ted Kennedy for a luncheon speaker. The writer from U.S. News & World Report sat at our table, and he had a copy of the speech. I asked him why he followed it when Ted was speaking, and he said that you can't trust these high-profile speakers. They sometimes . . . quite often . . . don't follow the printed script. He didn't here either!

New York, NY American Advertising Federation Convention(s) . . . during my era there were a couple of conventions in NYC. The Waldorf Astoria was the headquarters hotel, and a few from Bakersfield went. We stayed there. The speakers were top guys from leading advertising agencies . . . because most advertising agency principals were in New York. We did have some Walnettos with us, and stuffed them in the mouths of the lion statues in the main lobby. I guess the lions ate them, because they were soon gone! We were told that there was a three-hour boat trip around Manhattan, and there would only be beer and hot dogs. We decided to buy a douche bag and fill it with vodka. Someone had a carrying case that it fit in . . . a place to hold some ice, napkins, swizzle stick, glasses, etc. We took our "kit" onboard, and immediately went to the rear of the boat. We asked the deckhand for some chairs, and he said he couldn't do it. Andrew Jackson ($20) changed his mind. The word got out that "Bakersfield" had martinis, and all the top dogs came back to visit us. We poured them all a drink, and even offered a "mist" with some tool that came with the kit. It was memorable.

Regional AAF Conventions . . . were between the National Conventions. We hosted one in Bakersfield, and it went well. We were told that the members came to Bakersfield, and drank. I think we had 6 cocktail parties in three days. ** Ken Ramsey and I decided to go to the San Francisco regional meeting. We had long since resigned or got kicked out of any responsibilities, offices, or positions in the local or national AAF. At the San Francisco meeting we noticed that plenty of people had ribbons showing they were Board Members, Speakers, Officers etc. After a couple Ken and I decided we should get some ribbons too, so we went to a advertising specialty store close by the hotel. We got some 50 ribbons, like "Best of Show", "Usher", "Seventeenth Place" and many others. At the noon meeting we wore a badge with all these ribbons on it. Everyone laughed. We had extras, and offered them to members who didn't have a ribbon. It tells you something about those who ask for "1st Place", or "Eighteenth Place.

Trade Outs . . . Due Bills . . . Or as Capt. Sherwood called them . . . "Billy Do's" by whatever name are exchange agreements where you trade your product or service for another guy's. Over my lifetime I've traded out Sun Tan Lotion (Hawaii Tropic), funerals, "boob" job, gasoline, cars, clothes, groceries, restaurants, movies, cruises, airfare, hotels, dentists and doctors, carpet, painters, appliances, televisions, TV advertising, Disneyland, and who knows what else. ** When Ramsey first came to Bakersfield, he worked for the outdoor board company. He said they wanted to get a trade out in Las Vegas, so I connected him with Jeanne MaGowan at the Dunes. They got it, but it expired in one year . . . so Ken asked his boss if he could use the balance (about $7G's) before it expired. They said OK, so Ken got a big group of people . . . some 8 couples including us, the Vordermarks, the Wards, the Lymans, and others. We had the largest suite at the Dunes . . . it had three couches. On arrival Ken ordered two bottles of everything, a table full of goodies etc. The tip was $40.00. The whoopee cushion got action throughout the stay. We ate in the Dome of the Sea, Sultan's table, and the Top of the Dunes. At different times we all took care of signing the *big* checks . . . but they all ultimately went to Ken's account. We bought drinks and breakfasts for anyone in sight. It was a ball, but the tips damn near broke us. The final tab was over $6,000 . . . a record trade out! **The Sultan of Swap was Sol Gould in Los Angeles. He could trade anything, and often helped us in Vegas and Bakersfield. ** KWAC et al had a trade in Las Vegas with the Dunes. It was for room, food, and beverage. We got to know Lee Fischer and Jeanne MaGowan when we were in Las Vegas, and she let us trade in Bakersfield. For convenience she sent us a big bunch of "green cards." These saved her from sending us one every time we had someone going to the Dunes on our trade. I was loose about it, and some of those who got cards used them a number of times. Jeannie died in 1978, and in January 1979 we got a bill on the city ledger from the new owners for some $76,000. We informed them they had that much advertising coming. They asked for "hard" goods, so we would send them a $300 TV and charge them $1200. Somehow, I'm not sure how, over time it went away. She was evidently just chalking up charges to the city ledger and it obviously got out of hand . . . and we didn't know until the new owners came along. If the bill had been $7,000, I probably would have paid it out of fright. The tax consequences and music license consequences of the trades got lost in the wash, I hope!

Some Lake Powell excursions . . . and there were many. Lake Powell, in Utah and Arizona, is an interesting lake. It has some 1800 miles of shoreline and you can go up the many tributaries. It always looks like a three-mile lake, but when you get to the end you see a way to go farther. That repeats on and on. ** Judge Lund liked to go fishing and had a friend, Tommy Turner, who liked it too. We must have gone twelve or fifteen times. The guys would go in two trucks, and drag a ski boat. We would rent a houseboat, and go out for two or three days. It was fun, and the many different guys who went with us loved it. Needless to say we imbibed, and ate well. We would go to Mesquite, Nevada, the first night, and the only thing there was the Peppermill Hotel. We would eat at their gourmet restaurant, gamble a little, and leave early to get to Lake Powell before noon. It was really a break from the grind, and gave the gals at home a "rest" too.

On a couple of occasions, Pat and Milt Bade (Doris Lund's brother), Bill and Phyllis Owens, the Lunds, and Hopples rented three houseboats. All the kids went and it was a mob scene. We fished, water skied, camped on shore, and the whole gang had a great time. My Susan remembers three houseboats stopping in the middle of one of the areas and having a swim stop. It was wild. Climbing the rocks to get to old Indian ruins was educational, and going to Rainbow Falls was a real experience.

Whitewater rafting . . . I did it once. Somehow Howard Channell had about eight guys in his service club who were going on a whitewater trip down the Colorado River. He said they wanted ten for one raft, so I got Bill Ward (known as the "reverend" . . . but was really president of a bank in Santa Maria) to go with me and Howard's gang, which included George Serban and John Wilson (photographer). We went to Las Vegas, and the tour people picked us up and took us to Glenn Canyon Dam, the dam where Lake Powell empties into the Colorado River. The tour was on inflatable rafts, bound together with something and driven by an outboard motor. Off duty LA firemen were the so-called crew. The Old Woman of the River was a 75-year-old gal in leopard skin leotards . . . a legend on the river . . .

named Georgia Clark. It took 6 days . . . and we stopped every night on some beach or in a cave.

Some people had a real dish, but the Reverend and I used a dog dish. At about five o'clock they would give us a ration of blackberry brandy. I think it kept our systems intact.

The food was good, but mixed and slopped in a bowl. When you're hungry you'll eat anything. At eleven in the mornings they would give us a hardboiled egg. We were supposed to break it on our head because one of the eggs *wasn't* hard boiled! I never got that one.

We would stop and explore caves and interesting venues along the way . . . take a "bath" in the streams etc. Phantom Ranch at the bottom of the Grand Canyon was neat. The rapids were fantastic. When we came to a small "run" they would warn us to hold on. If it was bigger, they would call it a "hold on tight", and if it was a gigantic one (like Crystal or Lava) they would tell us it was an ". . . oh shit!"

We were told that if we fell out, just coast with the water and we would come to get you. A few of the passengers *did* fall out. **When going over a *really* big falls you could see the front of your raft over your head. I just held on for dear life and made it fine.

At the end of the trip they had a two-seated chopper that picked us up and took us up to the flat where a single-wing plane shuttled us back to Las Vegas. It was a great experience. Ours was one of the cheaper tours. The elite tours had "J" frame rafts, steak for dinner, ice, etc. We would have water balloon fights with them when we met on the river. I preferred our tour and our people. It was neat!

Some of our Bakersfield Haunts . . . we had a few. The kids and Cathie and I liked to go to the House of Don's on Union Avenue for dinner. They treated us nicely, and the food was good. It got tainted when the ladies of the evening started parading Union Avenue. The guys went there for lunch once in a while . . . Dave Vordermark, Dave Parker, Frank DeShong, et al. Those lunches were known to last 'til five o'clock. Ziggie, the bartender, got lots of action. **On New Years Eve when the gals were young, we would go to dinner at the Caravan Inn on Union Avenue by the Truxtun overpass. We would go early . . . while they were still decorating. The girls got dressed up nicely and they loved it. They always were given noise makers and stuff from the decoration stash. As time went on the gals had their own celebrations, and so did Cathie and I.

While on Driller we would go to the Tam O'Shanter. It was the only restaurant in our area. Along the line we went to the Bakersfield College football games. That's when the stadium was full! We attended shows at the new Convention Center. Early on the likes of Bill Cosby, Victor Borge, etc. performed there. **When we arrived in Bakersfield we went to the Pyrenees restaurant . . . our first taste of Basque food. Dinners were $1.50 with wine. We did go to other Basque restaurants, but the Pyrenees was our favorite. Al tended bar, Suzanne and Debby waited table. It was a Saturday night tradition for many years. **When the Blue Note was in action we went there quite often. It was classy, expensive, and good! It was also close. I may think of others, and if I do I'll insert them.

The Las Misiones Story . . . just by chance. Our radio stations had trips to Baja Mexico which we packaged with advertising schedules. Since the early 70's we would take groups to Cabo San Lucas . . . sometimes in the corridor between Cabo San Lucas and Cabo San Jose. They were five or six days, and clients loved them! In 1989 we were at the Posada Real on a tradeout. I was on the beach and struck up a conversation with a friendly Canadian. It was Vincent Carroll, and in the conversation he said that he was looking for a condo, but couldn't find one that he could afford so he would have to build one with a casita that he could rent. I asked him if there were any good ones, and he said the best were right across the street at Las Misiones. He also said that a salesman from there came over to the Posada pool bar for his afternoon aperitif.

About an hour later Bill Owens tapped me on the shoulder and asked if I would like to see the condos at Las Misiones. I asked Cathie, and she said "why not?" Four or six of our group went over to see the condos. Only Building Number One was built. Bill showed us the second floor condo (#122), which had tools and jointers working in it. They were making all the louvers for the project's doors etc. Bill explained the costs and we went back to the Posada. The next day some clients . . . like Dick Davenport . . . wanted to take a look, so we went back. Bill took us into the sales office where the sales manager was located. Somehow I asked Cathie if she was interested. She said "yes," if we can have one on the ocean. They said that #122 was available. I said that if they could have all the paperwork done by the time we left the next day, and could put the down payment on a credit card, we would take it. They did. I left a check for the balance of the down with Owens to use in 30 days. I then worked on covering that check when I got home.

Time went on, and in November 1989 they said that the condo was finished and the payments would start. I flipped the developer (Xavier Esquino) whether my payments would start in December or January. I won and started the payments in January and dealt with him for the balance. He discounted it a little and I paid him off in December 1991. A bunch of our friends and family came down at different times. It got crowded and people were sleeping on the couches, etc. The condo across the hall (#121) came up for sale, so I bought it . . . on the theory we would have four bedrooms, four baths, and a couple of kitchens, and that would be enough to accommodate everyone. Seems it was still crowded, and friends and family, who had come down before, wanted to come again.

By this time there was a homeowners association, and Paul Swoboda and I were on the Board. I met Paul when Jack Lund and I were having a drink on our balcony and he came by on his bicycle with his tee shirt tied around his leg. The best dog in the world, *Magic,* was with him. He asked if we could take him to the clinic. We took him . . . he got 40 stitches in his leg, and it only cost $40.00. Those were the days! He was down here while wife Marsha was working in Boulder. Marsha did quit her job and they have been coming down together ever since We got to know each other really well . . . and have been *best* friends ever since.

Cathie and I spent part of November for the HOA meetings, and January thru April at Las Misiones. The Board members were interesting, but Paul made it go. We fixed the place up, got a great manager, kept the dues low and did a lot of covert actions. That's Mexico! ** When Kak and Dewey Johnson were going to sell their condo, I had been diagnosed with prostate cancer, and thought I should have a first-level condo so I could wheel out and play gin with the gang. I bought #313 with that in mind.

We made some other good friends of other owners like Ken and Averill Fudge, John and Monique Scott, Liana McGee and Tom Kleinschmidt,

Marge & Don Molesky, Glenda and Ross Siegle, Dave and Audrey Green, Hank and Doris Pura, Sonia and Lou Waller, Deb and Doc Campbell, John Bossi, Cheri Gagnier, Jean Campbell, Miriam and Dave, Chile and Barb, Ed Diddle and Sandy Hadlock, Vince Turner, "Bo" Boveri, and of course the Twins (Bernie and Lenny).

So many others, both owners and renters, have made Las Misiones a real community . . . like David and Dale Hodges, Doris and Dwain Miller, Holly and Lloyd Rideout, Jack and Gilly Robson, Bernie and Marlene Konopinski and Ben and Eleanor Jensen et al. Of special significance are Carol and Jim Gallagher... our staff who helped at every venue. Great friends too! Some who haven't really gotten with the "group" are Steve and Eula Dale . . . and Bill Shephard . . . and Linda and Fred Scott. The Scotts were aloof, but are now in the "family". Others who live in different complexes or homes are around a lot too, like Ruth and Ian Falkner, Paul North, Dick and Judy Pasalich, Pip and Martin Roberts etc.

When the other condo on our floor came up to bat, I bought it from Nick and Pier Azcona . . . it is #123. Ken Freeberg sold me his condo . . . #213 . . . in 2005. I will probably get rid of that one, as they can all get to be trouble keeping them maintained.

During the first ten years we all played golf at the Fonatur 9-hole course adjacent to our complex. Until 1991 it was the only golf course in Los Cabos. **There were various operators of the restaurant at the Palapa. When one didn't want to return, we put it out to bid. One operator came in for three weeks. When his help showed up on a Monday, all the equipment was gone. Paul Swoboda was there, and didn't have many choices. Palapa John was the employee who showed up, and he asked if he could do it. Paul didn't have much choice, so he loaned John fifty bucks. John and his family worked hard and built the thing up. He is a tradition after ten plus years, and is really an asset to the complex.

When we moved into #122 we had a 180 degree view of the ocean. That started to diminish as hotels, time shares, and condos were being built. Los Cabos had caught on and buildings were being built all over. From one 9-hole golf course it went to a premier golf destination with six or seven fabulous courses and more coming. There are so many fabulous restaurants it's hard to decide where to go.

LIGA Mac is a local charity that I enjoy supporting. We have a charity "gaming" party every year. (LIGA Mac supports the poor children of San Jose.) Guests to the party bring "heavy" appetizers; I furnish booze and dessert, and we utilize all three condos on our floor to house blackjack tables, Texas Hold 'em tables, etc. The proceeds go to LIGA Mac. The dealer help is volunteer, and often sloppy! The whole complex and guests look forward to the party every year.

I was very lucky to find Bill Woodman, a jack of all trades. When something goes wrong with one of the condos, I call him. Through the years . . . with the encouragement of Cathie . . . and later Kae . . . we have continued to upgrade the condos. At November 2008 they were all in very good condition.

I brought some old cars down there to leave. When they first came, they looked very good. Cabo is full of new cars now . . . and new car dealerships. My CABO KAR (1985 Buick) was stolen and I gave 3 CABO (1993 Chevy) away to Joaquin, the neat English speaking mechanic who keeps them going. I still have ONE CABO (1985 Olds that belonged to Cathie's mother . . . the car that lived in Pinehurst NC for a few years, then at the Underwood Club in NY, and then was shipped west to Bakersfield and driven down to Cabo), CABO TOO (also a 1985 Olds that I got from good friend Don Brown), and GO4 CABO (a 1991 Cadillac limo in great shape that I got from Digger at Greenlawn Cemetery in Bakersfield.

Las Misiones has been a great "situation" . . . enjoyed by many over the years and a great place for R&R when Bakersfield is gloomy. I'm so glad I talked to Vincent Carroll on the beach that day in 1988. It was just by chance and it worked out *so* well!

The Underwood Club . . . a summer paradise. I was 8 years old when I first went to the Underwood Club. Uncle Russ Dwight (JD's grandfather) told my dad that he thought it might be good for my Mom to get in the fresh air. Dad had July for a vacation, so we drove up there. We fished every day, and had a wonderful time. My sister and I wrote nice thank you notes, and my parents were accepted by the other members. They played bridge . . . I carted groceries for the older ladies . . . and generally fit in. We were invited back the next year, 1939.

In the fall of that year a camp came up for sale, and my Dad bought it "sight unseen". In 1940 it was a thrill to go to our own camp and see what was there. There were two buildings and a garage. There were animal skins all over, a great bunkhouse/dining room, and we came there every summer from then on. Sal and Rip Coleman had it for many years after Dad and Janet decided to go to Michigan instead of Underwood. I think Janet *decided*. **When my sister Sal died, and then Rip died . . . Vicki Coleman (their daughter) got the camp and occupies it today.

I spent many summers fishing, playing ball, playing some golf, climbing mountains, and generally having a great time in cool weather. The years Mom was alive she had some of her friends from Wyoming visit. They loved it. Mom would have something for us kids to do all the time . . . pull taffy, make fudge, crank homemade ice cream, make a "food" cake, play fan-tan and other card games, pop corn, and even go to the movies in Schroon Lake.

There were a bunch of kids "in camp." Matt Davidson, Chuck McChesney, Bill Johnson, Rip Coleman, sister Sal and other friends and guests. When Cathie and I moved west to live, we didn't get to Underwood very much. As many as twenty years sneaked by with our going there only once or twice. Later I started taking more time, and our Bakersfield friends would come along for weeks at a time. It was a little inconvenient for Rip and Sal, and when the gal next door called me and asked if I wanted to buy her camp, it took a micro second to say yes. I knew it was the smallest camp of the seventeen that comprise the Underwood Club, but at least Cathie and I were in the ball park.

Many visited us that year, and we farmed them off to Perk Grant, sister Sal and Ann Kaufman's camps to sleep . . . after all, we only had two bedrooms, one bath, and a screened porch. It did have a separate woodshed and workroom and the first year they got lots of action.

Dirty Dottie Ramsey did curtains, Diny Dickerson did the carpets, and Deefy DeFay did a new septic tank. A lot of "D's" worked that summer.

Cathie said that we should build some bedrooms behind our camp on the property we owned. JD Dwight got us a builder and an architect. The architect sent the plans to us in Bakersfield that fall. He had designed something better than we had envisioned, so we told him to build it. We had no contracts. When they needed money, they called. That winter we went to see the ice cutting . . . stayed at Dwight's, and saw the framing for our new camp. We drilled the first water well, and therefore were able to winterize that camp. Those involved in building the camp were told to use their own judgment . . . and if they had a question, ask their wives.

When we arrived in the summer of 1985, we were thrilled. It had a big living room, a big kitchen with an island, all the appliances . . . including two dishwashers, and a dining table that would hold twelve people. It also had an attic, four bedrooms with baths including tubs, and an extra half bath for guests. It's the same today . . . with railings, paths to the lower camp, a deep three-car garage, and flowers all over. Cathie and I were really pleased with the way she furnished it . . . with Stearns & Foster mattresses yet!

Things about spending summers at Underwood were many. Some of the most memorable were working with Dudley Moylan as the ice and garbage men. That was when Cliff Fleury was the caretaker, and during the war. I think we made twenty-five cents an hour. In that gig we had to carry 50 lb. bags of coal to the furnaces which heated the water for the camps. (It is time to note that the Underwood Club had a "Delco" to generate electricity for the camps. You couldn't have an electric refrigerator, any electric motors, and only 40 watt bulbs. Lights were to go off at 10:00 PM. There was only one telephone and it was at the caretaker's house.)

Mr. Cleary paid Dudley and me to put up the flag in the morning and take it down at night. One time one of us had forgotten and left the flag up all night. Mr. Cleary went to bed early and got up a little late . . . so we just left the flag up. Not right, but easier!

The members got the word that we were keeping track of empty liquor bottles at the dump . . . Pig Pen Alley. We called it the liquor Derby. Members started taking their empty bottles to town to get rid of them. They didn't want to win our Derby!

The closest town was Elizabethtown . . . the Essex County Seat. I can recall the Windsor Hotel with a block-long porch; the Deershead Inn about the same size; the A&P down on Water Street where my mom . . . during the war . . . went in and said she wanted two of everything they had; the Log

Cabin Saloon on the river where you could see many *big* trout swimming around; Aubuchons Hardware Store where they didn't have a telephone and when we bought something on a credit card, they went outside and spent a quarter to get the purchase authorized.

The whole area has matured and grown . . . neat schools, roads, golf courses, grocery stores, auto dealerships, appliance stores, medical clinics, a great hospital, and the big government complex. It's still a small town, but well planned and developed.

Some bits and pieces of things I remember, in no particular order of importance (or chronology) were cutting my thumb the first year I was there . . . the scar remains; catching baseball for Rip Coleman, who was young but went on to the majors and pitched for the Yankees in the 1956 World Series . . . and who married my sister Sal; the bingo party in the Casino (where the chauffeurs used to party) on Dudley Moylan's birthday. He received a pan from someone for his home in Minneapolis and said that he didn't need it because he *had* four pans and only four burners; baseball games between Underwood Club and Profile Inn . . . the Colbert's cuties; seeing the ice cutting in the winter.

It was in the 80's when Don Brown, Sid Sheffield and I went up to watch the ice cutting. Most people thought we were going to the Super Bowl, so Ted Velguth delivered a big cake of ice to each of our wives and put it on the doorsteps . . . kinda funny.

More: carrying groceries up the hill before the current road to our camp was put in; going on Lake Champlain in McChesney's boat and seeing the first Polaroid pictures; the old Westport Inn; sister Sal dating Johnny McPhee, who was on the panel of the weekly radio show "20 Questions"; going "night crawling" at midnight with flash lights, and getting a can of worms . . . especially after it rained; putting minnows in every thing that held water in the Moylan house when Ted and Lena were arriving (we're talking every glass, pitcher, toilet, sink, tub, vase, bed pan etc.)

More: I remember Wednesday night pizza when a whole gang went to someone's house for cocktails, to Mountain Shadows for pizza, and back to someone's house for dessert. It was sort of a progressive party and cost everyone five bucks. The members' picnics at New Pond after the Labor Day annual meeting.

One night all the kids slept out at New Pond. Rip Coleman had to take a leak, and did it too close to Bill Johnson because Johnson said he thought it was raining.

More: Fishing with Dorothy Hayden Truscott (Dorothy Johnson then) at Moss Pond. We made all kinds of noise, but we caught three trout. She was teaching me to remember a string of nouns by strange associations. Our fathers and the caretaker were working the same pond, and didn't catch anything; climbing the fire tower on Nokomis Mountain, and talking to the Ranger; sleeping in the maid's room off the bunkhouse while Marg Webb was den mother to the gals in the bunkhouse.

Caretaker Cliff Fleury would come down to fire the furnaces for hot water. He had a pet fox, and it scared the ladies. Aunt Helen Raymond would cover her legs with newspaper. Cliff would tell her to turn it over because the fox had read that side.

More: Shopping trips to Mineville and Port Henry during the war on the dirt Tracy Pond Road; going to King Phillips Spring to get water and gasoline and buy pies from the restaurant; learning to drive LENA in the old hayfield and in the potato patch; putting down the original TV cable to the camps; fixing up the old barn; Mrs. Dunn losing her diamond from her ring while swimming in Nokomis Pond. Dad said she would never sink because she had built-in water wings.

More: The old wooden boats in the boathouses at Nokomis and at New Pond; learning to clean fish; learning to row a boat and paddle a canoe; playing hide and seek; going snipe hunting; putting out salt licks so the deer would come to our end of the Nokomis pond, our old boathouse which was torn down and the wood used to make all the flower boxes on Club buildings; the day Cathie and her sister Barbara went out to buy a rowboat. They ended up with a paddle boat to try. It was so good they went the next day and bought another one.

More: The 55-gallon drum filled with gasoline during the war to power the old 1930 Pontiac (Lena); restoring "Lena" in the winter of 1985 for

Dad's birthday. It went to Cincinnati and lived for a few years and then was shipped to Bakersfield. It is in good shape and in Cayucos at Susan's place . . . ready for some parades.

More: When the Nokomis Dam broke and dried the pond. They had it rebuilt *fast* before the Adirondack Park Agency got wind of it.

More: Serving as President of the Club and trying to make everyone happy. (Mary Graff was treasurer, and she was wonderful . . . a great help); On my watch I had the job of firing Gary Cole when the Club went down to one caretaker. More memories include the dinners at Perk's camp; Perk telling us about the old times and original owners; in modern informal times the Colemans had a "Formal" cocktail party . . . invitation said wear the best you brought; numerous cocktail parties and lobster dinners at our camp; gin games in the living room and out on the porch; the day that Cathie came to visit and my mother asked her if she could cut pie. She said "for Christ sake, who can't cut pie."

More: The day that the US dropped the atomic bomb and the Japanese surrendered, everyone was at the caretaker's house . . . but we were caught with our flagpole down . . . being painted; the RACCU (Royal and Ancient Croquet Club of Underwood) croquet tournaments.

More: Long time friend Dudley Moylan takes credit for my so-called financial ability. We went to the horse races at Saratoga when I was a young tad. He taught me how to read the Racing Form, and I won! He said that a good bet was to buy a ticket on the daily double. If you won the first race, you *have* a ticket on the next race.

More may come to mind, but those are a few! Underwood changes . . . but it doesn't! It is truly an oasis in this crazy world, and I feel fortunate that I have been able to enjoy it for most of my years.

OBSERVATIONS AND
MISCELLANEOUS DETAILS

On Missing the On-Ramp . . . Life is funny, and there are some people who have had every possible opportunity and somehow they didn't get traction. I consider it a waste of human energy. Most were bad choices, or irresponsibility . . . but they never really got on the On-Ramp of life. They may find it in the future . . . I hope so !

On Losing Things . . . We have all lost things, but the best policy is to find whatever it is before you know you lost it. A couple of cases in point. I was in San Jose del Cabo at a photo shop in a small shopping center. I got the pictures and decided to drive 12 miles to Cabo San Lucas to the Home Depot. I got what I wanted, paid with a credit card which I carry separately from my wallet, and returned home. On arrival someone asked if I had my wallet. I felt my back left pocket and it was empty. I told them "no!" They said someone had brought it to Las Misiones and it was in my condo. It turns out that Pip Roberts was getting her hair/nails done and Martin Roberts had come to pick her up. He found the wallet in the street . . . picked it up thinking he would never be able to find the owner . . . looked inside and saw it was mine. He returned it to my condo. I'm forever grateful because it would be "hell" to get it all replaced when in Mexico and heaven knows what would have happened if someone else had found it. I'm sure the $200+ would have been gone.

My second instance was in Bakersfield when I brought some stuff home from the office. My address books, the condo booking book, the closing statement for the #57 condo I sold in Tamarack Pines, some rolls of quarters, and some mail were in the box I used as a briefcase. I was late for something and I left it on the trunk of my car. I went out that Friday evening and while I was doing something in the garage on Saturday morning, one of the owners in Tamarack, George and Janice Holder, came by with a bag of "stuff." She asked if it was mine. I looked and it was. They had picked it all up knowing it was important to someone. All the stuff had fallen off the car trunk as I turned out of Tamarack Pines on El Portal Drive. Both the 3-rings were smashed. Truck and car tracks were over everything. I would have been crazy looking for any one of the items. It's much easier to find stuff before you know you lost it. I'm most grateful there too !

In life you meet some smart people . . . and I met a few. Bob Vance, who also missed the On-Ramp, is one of my very best friends. Part of this book is dedicated to him. He seems to know something about every topic. Just ask and he'll tell. ** Bill Andrews from my Amherst class and fraternity . . . also roomed at Harvard Law the first year. He is a Law Professor there now. Boy was he smart! ** Jack Frankel, former President of Cal State Bakersfield who now resides in New York City. He acts, studies cello, writes plays and savors the city. He comes to visit at Underwood in the summers with his neat wife Ursula. ** Mary Connelly Graff, a member of the Underwood Club in NY, who was a writer, editor, and even Society editor of the New York Times. ** Kingsley Ervin, a member of the Underwood Club in NY was headmaster at schools in New York City, Greece, and probably elsewhere. Great wit and too damn smart. There were probably others but I didn't catch the intellect. Sorry y'all !

The Big Band Era . . . When I was in high school, the Big Band era was at its peak. The Dance Band we had used stock orchestrations. Most stocks were written for 4 saxes, three trumpets, three trombones, piano, drums, and string bass. Once in a while you got a violin section, guitar part or a 5th baritone sax part. They had an intro, a brass chorus, a sax chorus, a jump and/or ad lib chorus and a fancy ending. They were fun to play. My Dad bought a used "book" from Ray Raymond who had a local big band and gave it up. A 'book' was all the parts for each player. That's probably how the jump tune "720 in the Books" got its name . . . the leader would number each orchestration and when they were playing a gig, the leader would call the numbers of the tunes that were going to be played in the next set. In looking over these parts, you could see some pencil markings that the player had marked on the copy. Billy Butterfield had played trumpet with this "book" and many of his marks were an octave higher than written. When I was going to attempt this project, I asked good buddy Chuck Cecil (from The Swingin' Years radio program) if he had a list of the Big Bands. He sure did. Somewhere in this writing is the list. It's hard to believe but I heard and/ or saw in person most of them. It was a great era and the *Big Band* legend still lives on. Thanks Chuck!

Coincidence Happens . . . and here are some that happened to me . . . in no certain chronology other than my trying to recall them. When we bought our first condo at Las Misiones, the salesman was Bill Owens. It turns out that he worked for us at our station in Seattle . . . doing a jazz show. I didn't find it out until months after we bought the condo.

Mike Reynolds, a roommate and fraternity brother at Amherst, was picking up Marsha Swoboda, who lived 4 blocks away in Boulder, Colorado, to go to their softball game. He played and managed . . . she played. She told him she wouldn't be at the next few games because she was going to the Caribbean with a Cabo friend, Ed Hopple. He asked if it was Radio Ed Hopple . . . and she was amazed when he told her that we were friends at Amherst and hadn't seen each other in 40 years. He has since passed away. He had a doctorate in something terribly academic, and taught at a number of schools.

While heading for the "john" on the island of Martinique in the Caribbean in the 60's someone yelled "Ed." It was Cut Halstead's mother. I had met her when visiting Cut in Buffalo. He was an Amherst roommate, fraternity brother, and a great friend. Thirty years later he passed through Bakersfield a few times and stayed with us. He's gone now, but I keep up with his wife Jimi with Christmas cards.

In the Caribbean on St. Maarten: Cathie and I were on a cruise. We were walking down the street and our next-door Driller Avenue neighbors, Ron and Lynn Reynolds, came out of a shop. He was chief mechanic for Burke Ford in Bakersfield, and they were on a Ford jaunt.** Then in Las Vegas Cathie and I went to the Frontier Lounge one night to see Ike and Tina Turner. Cathie spotted Tom Street and some other Buffalo men. They were supposed to be . . . and may have been . . . in Monterey playing golf. They weren't happy to see us, so we told them what happens in Vegas, stays in Vegas. I'll bet they fretted the rest of the trip.

When Cathie and I went to Minneapolis for a Thomas Family reunion, we were meeting each other and I said that we had just come from upstate New York. Guy asked where, and I said the Underwood Club, south of Keene Valley. Cathie's half-brother Guy Thomas asked if we knew Johnny Robertson. We said sure. He then told us that Johnny and Judy Robertson lived next door to them in New Jersey. Guy and wife Vivian had been up to Underwood. The Robertsons had a blue Jeep and would go to New Pond a lot. It would have been possible for Guy to be introduced to his half-sister Cathie right there at New Pond. The half-siblings didn't know each other at all. That was the reason Guy Senior promoted the Thomas family reunion.

Burt Farber was a known Cincinnati pianist. His son was in my high school class. In Las Vegas we went to the Desert Inn to see The McGuire Sisters . . . and HE was their accompanist. Fun to see him.

Speaking of Cincinnati, Marcia Goldsmith is the Director of the Wyoming School Foundation. I was talking with her and Las Vegas came up. She asked when I was there. I told her December 1958 to June 1961. She asked if I knew Lee Fisher. I said, "Sure . . . he had the same job at the Dunes that I had at the Flamingo. We gave each other comps and helped each other out." She said . . . "Lee was my brother!" It's a small world !

IF and WHERE Are They ??? Through life you meet a number of people. Some just pass through your life quickly . . . some leave footprints you never forget. I wonder where a few of them are . . . or if they're still above the grass. Some of them that left prints are:

JOE PEEPLES, a jingle salesman and great con man. He did time for selling equity in a British group that had a pill you can put in water and it made gasoline . . . ??? **ED MODKINS who was a funny black announcer early in the KWAC history (that was before we went Spanish.) ** MARJORIE ARTHUR, my kindergarten girlfriend. ** ANDY ANDERSON, JERRY WILKOFF, BOB MORGAN who worked at WAMF, the college Radio Station at Amherst. ** TOM MACKELFRESH, RAY SHARP, YATE DEER . . . all of whom I played with in grade school. ** VICTOR LISACK, a foreign student from England who went to grade school with us. ** KATHY KENO, a food demonstrator in stores for KENO in Las Vegas.

PROM QUEENS . . . I had the pleasure of dating MARGIE CRAMER in college, and she ended up Senior Prom Queen at Amherst . . . Vaughn Monroe was the orchestra. A gal at the University of Massachusetts needed a date for their prom (which was held in the Amherst College gym). I got talked into going with her by Phi Delta Theta brother Ted Nugent. She was good looking and she won queen of the Univ. of Mass. Senior Prom. Lionel Hampton was the orchestra.

JACK DAVIS, an Army buddy who helped Marty Rokeach drive our car west to the Tahoe Biltmore. The hotel was on the California-Nevada border, so he crossed it 7 or 8 times so that when he was asked if he had been to California, he could say 7 or 8 times. ** PAT CROW, came from San Francisco and married DAVE CROW. He was one of the owners of the Tahoe Biltmore. He died early, but she stayed in Crystal Bay and raised the kid(s) working at the school there. ** JUNE MASON, who with her husband George Mason (a good Army buddy of mine) came to the Tahoe Biltmore and worked. They subsequently worked in Las Vegas. He died young. They had two kids, and I think she went to work doing legal printing in Los Angeles.

CHUCK MOUNTAIN (the TV announcer on the soap opera Love of Life) and PAUL HAIGH, who worked at BBDO Advertising. They both helped in selling College Radio in NYC.

An UNKNOWN enlisted man who traded orders for me at Fort Benjamin Harrison in Indiana. I went to Fort Bragg in Fayetteville, NC and the other guy went to Vietnam. He lived in Fayetteville and wanted to go overseas. I was getting married soon, and this switch helped. I'm forever grateful. **Another UNKNOWN that made a difference was a gal in the front of the American Airlines check-in line at LAX. Four of us were going to St. Maarten for Christmas with the Cirella family. Mark was going to med school there. The line was so long it was out the door . . . I told the gals to go up to the gate, get in line, and go! . . . I'd get there somehow. I told the male check-in clerk that I was really late and he said too bad, I would miss the plane. No space later either. A gal at the head of the line pointed to me and said go ahead . . . she pointed a number of times. I checked in and got to the gate just as they were boarding. (No security searches at that time). As I was running I heard Meri, Susan, and Cathie say . . . "Here he comes!" We made it because of that gal. It would have been terrible if I'd missed it.

BEN NEIMS, a middle-aged salesman early in KWAC's history. He was smart, a great bridge player . . . but also a con man. He passed some bad paper and ultimately went to jail. We visited him and he was teaching prisoners and the warden how to play bridge. A real charmer.

SOL GOULD and BOB KELEM . . . were the Sultans of Swap (barter, due bills, trade outs, and as Capt. Sherwood called them . . . billy-doos). They were both real characters and got us a lot of goods and services we wouldn't have had a chance of getting otherwise. ** JIM EVANS, a funny TV manager who taught me the phrase . . . "Write if you get work!" He also did the "Frozen Owl Business Record".

GLEN MASINA, who handled Capital Airways trades, and a bunch of us got plenty of trips East because of him. ** KAREN SARS . . . who was a Rotary Foreign Exchange student from Norway who stayed with us in Bakersfield. She loved it there, and introduced us to Lynn Lebeau, who later ran the Williams Ranch for us. Lynn returned to finish college and stayed with us . . . even took the 17-day Christmas cruise on the Rotterdam with our family. Bernie Lebeau connected with her and we've all been great friends ever since.

Interesting Sayings . . . through life you hear a number of sayings . . . both original and stolen . . . and some of my favorites were from my parents.

Mom's Sayings . . . On opportunity = The time to take tarts is when they are going. **On problems = Trouble's not trouble if you can buy your way out. ** On economics = I vote for all the improvements in the poorhouse . . . and . . . God Bless the Rich! . . . and . . . My middle name was Pullman (on the towels she stole from a train) . . . and . . . If one is good, two is better. **On spelling = The "P" is silent as in swimming. ** On comfort = There's nothing too good to sleep in. ** On obesity = They call her Nearly 'cause she's all but(t). ** On cooking = Anyone can be a good cook if you have plenty of butter and prime rib. ** On labor = Work is the curse of the drinking class. She also said you have to pay to see the bright lights.

Other sayings included: There is honor among thieves; when as a kid I picked my seat she would ask if I was picking my seat to go to a show; when picking my nose, she would say "Get me a green one"; when cussing she would tell me to quit my cussing, it sounds like hell; someone who was really dressed up = The Grandest Tiger in the Jungle; and she always used the old standby . . . If you can't say something nice, say nothing at all.

Some other interesting facts about Mom . . . she financed a friend to start My Weekly Reader, which is in grade schools to this day; she played the bugle at camp, and still played until she got her false teeth; at camp she taught a one-armed camper to swim; Mom got kicked out of Smith College for smoking! Her father said that 6 months in Europe would be the same as a college education, and she did it; she and her older sister, Memaw, would spend hours tying bows with their toes. They got so they could do lots of things toe-wise. Mom was always sick, and was the first on sulfa drugs and the first on antibiotics. Even feeling bad, she was a catalyst for getting all kinds of fun things going. She died at age 52 of multiple cancers. Sister Sal followed in her footsteps, both as a catalyst and dying of cancer.

Dad's sayings . . . If I ever go into government, I want to be in charge of Indian Affairs. I've never had an affair with an Indian. **Jesus asked for Moses to come forth, but he came fifth and was disqualified. ** It takes class to drive a Chevrolet when you can afford a Cadillac. ** Asked if he ever slept with a redhead, he said "not a wink!" ** Some things were built on a bluff, and run on the same plan. ** Those architects MCVIC and MCVII did plenty of buildings. ** I don't want to be found wanting when weighed.

When my grandson Eddie Roberts was 2 years old, Dad described him as a one-man gang. ** About eating he said we were "putting on the feed bag." ** On relieving himself, he would say he was going to shake his grates . . . or let Shorty out . . . or I'm going to cast my vote for Roosevelt! ** On doing something stupid he would say it was like taking a ham sandwich to a banquet. **On economics he said that inflation is a terrible thing, operating capital is a wonderful thing, and stay as far away from debt as you can. ** He believed that youth IS too good to waste on children, the Golden Years ain't for Sissies, and he would see you in the funny papers.

Other neat sayings gleaned on the road were . . . LES WEBB who would leave a house and say . . . thanks for inviting me over to impress your friends. He also said that when the cat's away the mice act like rats. ** FRANK DeSHONG would say that he could stand any kind of hurt but pain. ** DOTTIE RAMSEY wonders why there are so many more horses' asses than horses. ** VINCE TURNER says that what little he remembers, he'll never forget! **My Uncle Hall would say that I don't want some, I've got any. ** JACKIE GAUGHAN said that people are more consistent than horses. If it's in them, it will show. ** IAN FALKNER says there is always enough for the needy . . . but never enough for the greedy. He also said that drinking gin makes him break out in handcuffs. ** TIGER NOVAK describes something as . . . Fine as wine and mellow as a cello. He also said that money on the wood makes the betting good. ** PERK GRANT described drinking as getting a little tiddly . . . or she was seeing double and feeling single. She also said behind every successful man there is an astonished woman . . . and when she was alone she always wanted someone to stay with her. She said she didn't like herself enough to stay alone.

When MARTY ROKEACH was asked if he took a shower, he'd say "Why, is one missing?" ** TRICE HARVEY via DAN PANERO agree "you can't fix stupid!" ** GORDON SHERWOOD described a pregnant lady as having been bit by the trouser bug. ** The NY advertising community stated that in advertising one half works and the other half doesn't. It was their job to find the half that worked. About advertising they also said that the people aren't much but you meet a lot of interesting money! **DON DOBSON on being down . . . said he had to reach up to grab bottom. ** MEGAN TOWNSON on exiting someplace says she is going to make like a tree and leave . . . I'm off like a prom dress . . . I'm going to make like a hockey player and get the puck out of here. ** DENNIS CORBETT uses my check slogan "it's only money". ** KAE BABCOCK tells me to piss up a rope. ** FRED SCOTT said his father told him that if you couldn't help someone, don't hurt them. **TV weatherman LLOYD LINDSAY YOUNG says it's better to be a has-been than a never was. ** When ED DIDDLE gets fished when playing gin, he calls it a Moose Call. ** PAUL NORTH said that life is like a roll of toilet paper . . . the closer you get to the end, the faster it goes.

KIB ROULETTE said to leave your coat in the car and have your first drink on the hat-check girl. ** PAUL SWOBODA says you can't win 'em all if you don't win the first one and also says that if the dog hadn't stopped to dump, he would have caught the rabbit. "Joke 'em if they can't take a f—." ** Night club comedian JOE E. LEWIS said . . . I follow horses and the horses I follow follow horses . . . and night club icon SOPHIE TUCKER said that she trades her men tit for tat . . . and she's entitled to a lot of tat for what she has to give. She also said that she had been poor, and she had been rich . . . and *rich* is better ** FRANK TINDLE's advice on life: He said to arrange your time so it's your own. It's the only thing that's really yours . . . and don't take life too seriously or you'll spend all your time crying. Cathie and I were just married and it went in both ears and out the other. As time passed I found it to be SO true!

TOM KLEINSCHMIDT states that you can't intimidate someone who doesn't give a shit. **SHERRIE McMURTREY, when she had received poor service, says that she was treated "shitally". **STEVE McCALLEY says opinions are like assholes . . . everybody has one. He also says that you have to have patience, or become one. **Homer Simpson via JEFF SWOBODA insists that alcohol is the cause of, and the solution to, all life's problems. **Those who say you can't take it with you always ask if you ever saw a U-Haul behind a hearse. **DWAIN MILLER, when losing at gin, says he's being beaten like a red-headed stepchild.**CLIFF FLEURY, the long-gone caretaker of the Underwood Club would talk about something, and then summarize by saying "that's the 'it' of it!"

Some Things I Dislike . . . I like almost anything . . . and eat almost anything . . . but here's a list of items that I can remember that I don't like: coconut, soggy corn flakes, basketball, opera, gross grammar, exercise, and intense academics. There may be more.

The Best Palindromes I Know = "Never odd or even.", "A man, a plan, a canal, Panama" and "racecar." I also like "noon" and "poop".

The Funniest People I ever met . . . were good story tellers, could use dialects, and were always funny. Some were my Uncle Hall (Dad's younger brother), Don Waterbury (an ad salesman in NYC); Bob Christianberry (salesman—his father was NYC Postmaster); Bill Foulks (an announcer in Bakersfield); Matt Davidson (from Underwood and Amherst); Dottie Ramsey (long time friend and cohort); Pier Ascona (from CA and Cabo); Dave Maxwell (TV manager) . . . and quasi-subtle professionals like Myron Cohn, Sheckey Green, Bill Cosby, and Victor Borge . . . among others.

People I Shook Hands With . . . During my life I have met some interesting people. I shook hands with Dwight Eisenhower in Cambridge, Mass when he was running for President. **Richard Nixon was in Bakersfield for a political rally . . . he was running for Vice-President and had a press conference at the Hill House. About 40 press were in the room, and he shook everyone's hand. As everyone knows, he did become President. **I was invited to the White House for a meeting of "minority" owned radio stations, and we all got to meet Jimmy Carter. Incidentally, I was going to steal an ashtray at the reception, but they were plain . . . so were the napkins. They were the quality you get in the dollar store! **I touched Pope John Paul's hand in Los Angeles, when he turned the opposite way that most people thought he would turn. It was at a speech for media at the Universal Sheraton. After the speech, he went down the roped off aisle to thank TV and other photographers. Most thought he would turn right, but he turned left and there I was. Ken Ramsey was with me. Later at Tony Roma's restaurant, Ken asked me if I was going to wash my hands. I said "sure . . . I don't know where he's been." That audience had a ton of celebrities . . . with spouses . . . like Loretta Young, Dom Deluise, Bob Hope, Danny Thomas, Marlo Thomas, Ricardo Montalban, Danny Kaye, and the likes. ** George Bush Sr. was at an Ad Club meeting in Washington, and he shook everyone's hand too. **I met Ronald Reagan at the dedication of Cal State Bakersfield. He was Governor of California, and went on to be President. I was with groups that he attended, and saw him a number of times. **I met President Ford when he came to Bakersfield to check out the Elk Hills Petroleum reserve. All the press got to meet him. That was the day that my Dad and Janet came to Bakersfield. The big crowd and Air Force One were at Meadows field. Dad thought it was nice of me to give him such a big reception. That was Dad!

My Favorite Toasts . . . There have been many, but my favorite for weddings was when I stood up and lifted my glass . . . and said "*fornication*". I would then pause . . . while the audience mumbled, laughed, or whatever . . . and then I would say "For an occasion like this, we wish the bride and groom happiness etc. . . . ."** The other one I liked was a toast before dinner at Slug's Place in Underwood. Art and Polly Pepin were there as guests of Pete and Ann Kimball. Art and Pete had been in the War together, and hadn't seen each other in plenty of years. Art bought the golf course in Westport, NY. Their meeting at the golf course was one of those unforgettable moments. At dinner Polly lifted her glass and said . . . "Friends may come and friends may go . . . and friends may peter out you know, but I'm your friend through thick or thin . . . peter out or peter in."

Bumping into the Right People and Timing . . . sometime things just don't work out and then someone crosses your path that can easily fix it . . . or timing is just right in a situation that changes your life. ** My sister wanted to go to Oberlin College in Ohio. Her advisor said she couldn't ever get in. She then applied and was accepted at Rollins in Florida, and planned to go there. Prior to her going to Rollins she was on a trip West and was doing a square dance with an older guy at Crater Lake Lodge on Mount Hood, Oregon. He asked her about going to college, and she related that she wanted to go to Oberlin . . . but was told she couldn't get in. He said that he was a trustee of Oberlin and if she wanted to go, she would be in. She went to Rollins and loved it.

When we lived on Elm Street in Bakersfield, the Ramseys gave me a phone booth for Christmas. They saw it in someone's back yard and asked them if they wanted to sell it. They did. I wanted a coin toll phone (it would be free but look good to put in the pool area. I asked Tom Jarvis, manager of the phone company in Bakersfield, and he said he would try. Months went by. I was in Miami Florida at a Better Business Bureau conference, and had a few drinks with a guy from the Ohio Bell Telephone Company. I asked him about it, and he said his good friend was V-P of Pacific Telephone and he would call him. Three days later Tom Jarvis called me and asked what it was that I wanted. I told him and the next day he had one. He told me that if I needed help installing it, *only* call him. I did and a couple of days later Cathie called me at work and said that there were three phone trucks at the house and Tom Jarvis was there. I came home (a 4-minute trip) and they were finishing it up. One of the trucks was a pickup and driver that they use to do covert work . . . like stringing cable through chain link fence. He was a funny guy . . . but they got it working. Again I was told if there was any problem, Call Jarvis, The next day Jarvis called me and asked if I would drop a note to the V-P in San Francisco and say that all was taken care of to my satisfaction. I did, but the guy from Ohio Bell made it possible.

On timing, it was by chance that Mr. Hecht was in town from Atlanta and came to the house for dinner at graduation time. The trip with him around the country really extended my horizons.

When we lived in Las Vegas, Cathie and I were in Seattle visiting the Sherwoods. They encouraged us to stay longer, but we came home and the next day Dr. Hardy from the Las Vegas Hospital called and said we have a baby girl for you. It was Lori!.

Things of Old That I Miss . . . Things and People . . . HUSMANN'S big
red can of potato chips which was always in our kitchen. ** WHEELMAN's
REST . . . a restaurant in Reading Ohio . . . close to Wyoming . . . where
they had the best steaks and rye garlic rolls. It was only open evenings, and
the waiter(s) did lunch in Cincinnati where the judges ate. If you had a
traffic ticket, you would hand it to the waiter with a $20 bill and somehow
it was taken care of the next day. ** The BLUE NOTE . . . a great restaurant
in Bakersfield. Son-in-law Mark Cirella was the bar manager there when
he married Lori. He's now Doctor Cirella. ** PIETRO'S . . . an Italian
restaurant in Cabo San Jose that Cathie and I loved. Bruno ran it, but it
fell on hard times with the all-inclusive hotels. ** The OCEAN VIEW
from our Condo at Las Misiones. It was 180+ degrees . . . with all the
building, and more to come, it is now about 30 degrees. ** The TRAILER
PARK in Cabo San Jose . . . Right on the beach and 2:1 drinks on Sunday
afternoons. ** PURDY'S ELM TREE INN . . . in Keene, New York has
been closed for a few years, but if it opened it would be full. I was Monty
Purdy's first bartender . . . and it was a great experience. The food, drinks,
prices, and service have always been fabulous.

About Purdy's . . . The summer of 1949 I was lucky enough to get the
bartender's job there. Monty was hunting for a young guy to work days.
Ed Orth from Underwood used to sell restaurant and bar supplies for
something to do. He knew me and recommended me to Monty. It was a
great experience, and Monty taught me a lot about the bar business which
stood me in good stead along life. He used hot water to make ice because it
froze faster. We used club soda to clean the bar . . . it really worked.

My mother said she would pay for my first five mistakes. She only had to
buy one, when I made a brandy Alexander with applejack. ** After I had
been there a few days, Monty told me that if a customer was on his/her
way to Lake Placid and asked for a glass of red wine . . . I should put it in a
wine glass like the one he was holding. Charge 65 cents for it. If a worker
came in and asked for a Sneaky Pete, put 3 ice cubes in a highball glass, fill
it with the same wine and charge 25 cents.

There was a daily customer named Frank Vagnarelli (sp?) who did the clay
tennis courts at the Ausable Club and elsewhere. He drank Ballantine Ale.
He was a character and all the customers would want to buy him a drink.
After a couple of weeks he got to know me and said that when they offered

to buy him a drink, pull out a Ballantine and put it under the bar. When he had five or six stacked up, he would buy the house a drink. I'd give them what they wanted and put his "stash" back in the cooler. He called that Scientific Drinking!

Monty had some "Kit-Cat" clocks. They were cute. Many times a day customers would ask about them and if we sold them. Monty said to charge $25.00 and dicker if I had to . . . but don't sell for less than $12.50. He had paid $8 for them. I had a line about getting a commission on them (I didn't!). I'd tell customers I would waive my commission and they could have one for $20.00 . . . more or less depending on how I had pegged them and how much they wanted one. I never got less than $16.00.

The beer salesmen would come in and put a buck or two in my "education jar." The Utica Club guy was the best. We sold lots of beer, and I would figure out which brew I wanted to "push." People would come in and say they wanted a beer, I would start naming what we had, and when they were about ready to say "yes" . . . I'd slide in Utica Club and they would take it. If they had a second one, they took another Utica Club. It was challenging, but I could unload an extra case of almost any brand on a shift. ** I bought Ronnie (Monty's son) his first Cub Scout Uniform. In later years when we started to come back to Underwood, we would often go to Purdy's to eat . . . summer or winter. It had been enlarged and remodeled and Ronnie ran the joint . . . and followed his Dad's good advice. Wear a tie! Then they know who's boss! Daughter Stacey tended bar (when not teaching). Ronnie's wife Katie worked (when not teaching), as did Ginny, Norm, Diane, Gladys et al.

They always had charity raffles, and one was a 50-50 raffle for the Keene High School graduates to take a trip to Hawaii. I think there were five graduates. There were about forty $100 squares and I bought one or two. After the drawing they called me in California and said I had won. I told them to give a grand to the graduates so they could do something they couldn't do otherwise . . . and I'd pick up the other grand when I came to Underwood the next summer. They liked that! ** During the 1982 Winter Olympics in Lake Placid, the press was giving the area a terrible time about parking. People parked at the Keene Airport and were bused to the events. I called Monty and asked him how it was . . . and he said it wasn't bad at all. He gave his upstairs to the State Troopers for R&R, and they said the problems were vastly overstated.

St. Luke's Episcopal Church . . . being well entrenched in the Episcopal Church in Las Vegas, the Sherwoods and Hopples went to St. Luke's on Mt. Vernon Avenue in Bakersfield. It was close to our house. They had the beginnings of a building program. Three years after we joined, they built a new church. Before that, the services were held in the recreation room. We sat on folding chairs. The physical plant wasn't much, but the people were *great* and we stayed. This is where I met the Williams family, and ended up buying Williams Ranch in Pioche, Nevada from them. I still belong and go there when I'm in Bakersfield. Gordon and I had helped build an Episcopal church in Las Vegas. Gordon's brother, John Sherwood, sold church pews. He equipped the Las Vegas church, and we enticed him to sell us the old pews from Vegas. They are still there and look pretty good. I bought the carpet for the new church building, and it lasted 40 years. We started with Father Ashbee, then John Wilcox, John Galligan, Terry Burley and a few others along the way. I was on the Vestry a couple of stints . . . and I was Senior Warden, Junior Warden, Treasurer etc. The church has grown, and now Father Jack Estes has three services on Sundays . . . The traditional at 9:00 am which I attend; the Modern at 11:00 am with guitars etc., and the Spanish at 1:00 pm. It is growing and in good financial shape, in that 35 years ago we bought some adjacent property. It sold for well over a million dollars . . . and we still have some of the land left for parking. There are two other Episcopal Churches in Bakersfield. Both are much closer to my present house than St. Luke's, *but* I drive across town 'cause I call it home.

My Wyoming School Teachers . . . I started with Miss Lumbarger (sp?) in kindergarten, and had Miss Lepp in 1st grade. Then Miss Shifflet in 2nd, followed by Miss Hamilton in 3rd grade. Then came 4th grade and Miss Schultz. Miss Brigode and Mrs. Hiller were my 5th grade teachers. That's when they taught us to change rooms for one class. Mrs. Hiller taught geography. Miss Brigode's brother was Ace Brigode, the well known big band leader (he was the house band at the El Rancho when we moved to Vegas.) Mrs. Anderson and Miss Brand shared us in sixth grade. When I/we got to seventh grade, we had Mr. Betz for history and civics, Miss Williams for Latin, Miss Culp for Spanish, Miss Mittendorf for English and Mr. Bush for math. I forget who taught biology and physics. The high school principal,

Mr. Bradbury, taught chemistry. Mr. Letzler taught band and chorus; and Mr. Naugle taught algebra, geometry and other subjects mathematical. I/ we went K thru 12 in the same building.

It was a good education, and the school has a fine reputation to this day. They had neat events, like the May Fete, the chocolate sales, the paper drives, junior and senior proms, plays, band concerts, forensic debates, honor society, and naturally there were all sports teams. I used to make some coin selling ice cream and candy in the stands at the basketball games. It was good experience, and I think I learned a lot about people. Finally there was graduation! I'm proud to have gone there. My parents went there. It was a great place to grow up . . . village atmosphere and almost everyone knew each other. My high school class had about forty in it, and a third had gone there in the same building K thru 12. Practically everyone went to college.

The Williams Ranch Episode . . . in Pioche, Nevada . . . The family had been going to St. Luke's Episcopal Church from the time we got to Bakersfield. The Williams family went there also. Somehow I heard that they had a guest ranch in Pioche, Nevada, that they were going to sell. Cathie and I had liked Nevada, so we took some friends to the ranch to look it over. I guess I loved it . . . I'm not too sure about the rest of the family, but they went along with me. It was a long way from Bakersfield. It was some 400 miles thru Las Vegas, Caliente, into Lincoln County, thru the "city" of Pioche and then some seventeen miles north towards Ely.

The ranch had an air strip that was over a mile long. The main building had a restaurant, bar, kitchen and walk-in cooler, and was pretty well equipped. There was a building that had four bedrooms in it, and a stand-alone cabin that could house a small family. There was a pond, some heavy equipment for grading, a small barn, and some lots in the valley which various people owned. In general it was old Western atmosphere.

We decided to buy it . . . and did. We engaged Lynn & Rob Jolley, Dan and Patty somebody, and Mike Collins to work the ranch. I traded lots of stuff, and we upgraded the ranch. Harold Meek at Threeway Chevrolet loaned us a cargo truck when we needed it. Wally Tucker sold me a new small Datsun pickup truck cheap! The ranch got to be in pretty good shape. I even bought two slot machines to make it feel like it was in Nevada. I still have those machines.

Many people liked the dining room. Lawyers and judges who worked the famous courthouse in Pioche would stay at the ranch and decide the cases at *our* bar. The local telephone company would come often, as did others, and a few paying groups would come. Andy Hoover, President Herbert Hoover's grandson, was a mining engineer at the gold mine close by, and he came over quite often. My friends and I would fly up for a day or two with pilots Chuck Monk, Warren Thompson, and others.

Bill Thomas came up while he was running for California Assembly. He helped us revive three or four trout of the bunch we brought from Utah to stock the pond. Bill later became a US Congressman, head of the Ways and Means Committee, and even got the Bakersfield Airport named after him. Quite a career for a Bakersfield College teacher!

Williams Ranch was a great experience and the family and many friends had a lot of fun there, but it was far away from Bakersfield, and it was not really financially viable. Maybe that's because we had so much fun! Anyway, after three or four years we decided to sell the ranch. I took a classified ad in Sunset Magazine, and someone answered . . . came to the ranch . . . and bought it. I had paper, and they finally decided to quit, so it was sold to a modern religious order from Phoenix, and I got paid. They used it as a retreat for a few years and then I think it was sold to a Las Vegas Corporation that uses it for corporate retreats etc. At any rate, it was fun . . . expensive for me and the government . . . but an adventure I wouldn't trade for anything. Much like the Army . . . but I wouldn't do either one of them again.

The History Of Aspiring Tycoons and Toastmasters . . . (a.t.&t) . . . "No Service to Anyone." When the Blue Note Restaurant was in bloom, they had a few Cigar Nights. You would go there, pay $99.00 and smoke cigars, drink, and have a good dinner. Many enjoyed it. After the Blue Note closed, I was in Mike Allen's office one morning and he said that we should look into starting another cigar night someplace. I suggested the Pyrenees Restaurant. We talked for a while and decided that would be good. I came up with the name of the group, we settled on the slogan (No Service). It finally boiled down to having it three nights a year . . . during off "party" times. We would get sponsors for the bar (KMAP did the first one), have 69 members, have a 69-second speech to find out who would sponsor the bar next time.

The third Wednesday of February, June, and October were picked as the dates. All 69 members would get a calling card and be an Executive Vice-president. We would have only one CEO, and the first one was Harold Meek. All members would have a number. The number 69 went fast! It cost members roughly $125 a year . . . a little more now . . . for all three meetings. That's not bad for three events with an open bar, free cigars, and a great Basque dinner with three meats.

We met for years at the Pyrenees, and then they changed ownership. The new owners treated us poorly one night, and so we decided to move to the Noriega Hotel . . . famous for Basque food and service . . . and it's only a half a block away from the Pyrenees.

We still meet there and are *very* pleased with the way they treat us. We allowed guests for $35, and we have a bunch every meeting. Limos crowd the street on at&t night. At the present I'm the guru. I don't know why people like it, but they *do*. It is a great mix of people, from the symphony conductor to half-ass politicians. Jack Turnbull coordinates it and does a neat job. 17th Street Cigar Store furnishes the cigars at a great discount, and various members take turns sponsoring the bar. Members bring gifts to raffle off from a hat that everyone puts his/her calling card in. We're going on our thirteenth year.

Mike Earhart flies in from Texas to join us. He ran the Outback Steak House in Bakersfield before being transferred to Texas. Others come from a distance . . . and sadly a number of members have passed away. The spaces are filled quickly from the waiting list . . . Assistant Vice Presidents . . . or as we call them, "Ass members". It all works out well, and is easy to do. I like that!

Gourmet Dining . . . not often, but there were two very opposite groups that I was a part of. The first was a day group headed by Jack Baird, a church friend of mine, and a member of the East Bakersfield Rotary. He would organize a luncheon a couple of times a year. He would make special orders at the Great Castle on Union Avenue. We often went to the Bakersfield Air Park on Union Avenue. It included lots of booze and courses and lasted three or four hours. Some of the members were Dave Vordermark, Harold Meek, Larry Radanovich, Al Goodman, George Whiting, Frank Ghettzi, Lloyd Plank, and a few others from the East Rotary Club. It was always a grand occasion. Often times members would bring fish they had caught, or venison they had gotten and the place would cook it to perfection. Often we could bring guests, but in limited numbers. There were usually about a dozen "players".

My other experience in gourmet dining was when Sid Sheffield and the Four Seasons decided to have a quarterly gourmet dinner at one of our houses. Sid took a menu from the front cover of Bon Appetit magazine and assigned which dishes each couple was supposed to bring. I remember Cathie spent $100 on a cake to look exactly like the picture. It was unique, and the table settings and meals were very authentic. Needless to say, wine was consumed at dinner after a few cocktails. The evening was something to look forward to unless Sid gave you an impossible assignment. Even then, it was fun!

A Short Bout with Skiing . . . I had never skied, but the gals got involved at Carden School on some skiing trips. They talked us into going to June Lake and trying it. Cathie and I enjoyed it, but were not very good. The Lunds were much better. We all did ski at various places, including Mammoth, June Lake, Shirley Meadows, Park City, Banff, Lake Louise, and Sunshine (in Canada); Whiteface Mountain at Lake Placid, Squaw Valley and others at Lake Tahoe, a few in Vermont, and some I forgot. As the kids went away to school, discretion became the better part of valor, so Cathie and I gave it up. It was fun while it lasted. Now skiing to me is **S**pending **K**ids **I**nheritance.

Community Involvement . . . both Cathie and I were involved. She loved volunteering at Mercy Hospital, and had 35,000+ hours when she passed away. She didn't even count the weekly volunteer hours she spent at admitting. She also did Junior League, St. Luke's Church, and the Cancer Society. She did it because she wanted to. She also made it a point to work at all the special events at the kids' schools, and she went to everything the gals were involved in. I did my best to do that too, and did pretty well. ** I did a lot, because I wanted to and because it is part of the broadcasting and advertising game. **I was President of KMAP, Inc. and the radio stations; on St. Luke's Church Vestry, and Senior Warden; Kern Safety Council; Bakersfield Advertising Club; Campfire Girls; Volunteer Bureau; Better Business Bureau; Southern California Broadcasters; Bakersfield Chamber of Commerce; and at&t club. I was a director of Mercy Hospital and the Mercy

Hospital Foundation. I was chairman of the Cal State Advisory Board and Chairman of the CSUB Foundation, and remain a lifetime member.

I was on the homeowners board at the Underwood Club and Las Misiones . . . president a few years during my membership. The same is true of Bakersfield North Rotary Club. I also served a term as the *first* president of Rio Bravo Tennis Ranch. There were others but I can't remember them. It all helped in my business . . . and made Cathie and me feel good about returning something to the community that had been so good to us.

The Economic Bordello Christmas Lunch . . . as previously referred to in the New York, after the army, section of this book. The beginning is described there but I think it needs a little more detail of sorts. At this writing we have planned the 56th meeting of the clan. At the Capital Grill in New York City . . . on 42nd Street just off Park Avenue. There were about 20 at the beginning, and we're down to about 6. It was held in New York for many years, and many years at the Terrible Tehran Restaurant on West 44th Street. That may be off, but it doesn't make any difference. We then moved it to a room at Keen's Chop House somewhere on West 36th St. and it was there for a long time. I went to the lunch every year . . . maybe I missed a couple, but not many.

The individuals had spread out all over the country, so Bob Vance became the coordinator. It was transplanted off and on to Baltimore and Philadelphia. As the group "shrunk", it seemed more important to the remaining members to get together and talk about old times. In the last few years Kib Roulette has coordinated it . . . and we have gone to great restaurants. It is usually a four-hour lunch; a bit shorter if they need the room for something else. My favorite story is/was when Pete Kimble was with us, and we went to one of his favorite haunts for a few more and maybe dinner. There was a drunk there and somehow he poked me and I took a cut at him and he punched back. It cut my lip, and when I told the family about it . . . they said they were proud. They knew I had never been in a fight. The management took no time in kicking the other guy out of the place and buying us a drink.

At one of the lunches in the bar after the four-hour lunch . . . another drink *always* seemed like a good idea . . . Bill Irvine and I got to talking about "an Ed Brandt". We finally determined that "his" from West Virginia was the same as mine from Underwood. We all had known each other for 30 or 40 years but didn't know that Bill and Ed knew each other. In vino veritas . . . or something like that! A year or so after that all three of us went to Jim Brandt's wedding in San Francisco.

Some Letters That Missed the Circular File . . . and got saved. I'm not sure why. One is a letter that Cathie wrote to her parents asking them to come get her at summer camp. She must have been about 10 years old and hated the camp; a letter from my Dad sent to me on my 20th birthday, enclosing a check for $1000. He was paying off a bet that I wouldn't drink or smoke until I was 20 years old. He said he didn't want to be wanting when weighed. The bet was for $1000 or a Chevy Convertible. When we made the agreement, the cars were about $900. When my 20th birthday came, they were $2500 and he said he hoped that it was OK if he took the option. It was because I had a car.

Also a letter from Mr. Hecht saying that he didn't think the Tahoe Biltmore Hotel was a good idea for me . . . sleeping with dogs you get fleas; the letter that Mike Ramirez at KWAC wrote to Gordon Sherwood offering to buy his stock in KMAP, Inc; a letter from Tom Wyman, president of CBS, saying he wished I was there to help him; one from my Uncle Clark (Papaw) telling how Memaw died and how she considered me her son after her son Brice died as a youth; a postcard from Bob Vance saying that all the cigarette companies had cancelled schedules, and that it looked like we were out of biz.

I also have a letter from California Lt. Governor Mike Curb thanking us for the event we held for him at our house; a thank you note from Elton Rule, President of ABC Television . . . I'm not sure why; one from Howard Bell, President of AAF congratulating me on getting the Ad Club Silver Medal; many letters to my Dad congratulating him on becoming president of Stearns & Foster, and many others for being elected a director of the 5/3rd Bank; one to Cathie and me from Eppa Rixey (Cincinnati Reds pitcher and in the Baseball Hall of Fame) about Underwood; the letter that Rip Coleman wrote to Dad explaining why he wanted to retire from baseball; a number of the kids' letters that we bound in a book and gave to them for Christmas 2007.

Cruises and Trips . . . we *did* get around! I am taking the liberty of identifying the trips and cruises we took, but I just can't remember the exact order. With that in mind, I'll just list them as best I can. The first adventure I had on a "big ship" was when I was about 6 years old. My parents and I took the Island Queen from her dock in downtown Cincinnati to Coney Island . . . an amusement park just outside Cincinnati. It was my first amusement park adventure too, and we rode the ship back to the landing in the city. The trip took about 30 minutes one way, and the ship could hold 800+ people. I think it was free to try to get people to the park

When I was 10 the family was returning from Underwood, and we took the Lake Erie ferry from Buffalo NY to Cleveland OH . . . it took the night and we even had a stateroom.

In 1963 I took a Windjammer trip in the Caribbean. Prior to it I had attended a Spanish Language Radio convention in Dallas. I chomped on a piece of ice and broke a front ceramic crown. All I had was a nail hanging out, but the hotel aimed me to a medical building a block away. I just picked a dentist, went to the office, asked if he was a sailor. The nurse said he was, and just then he came in the back door. I explained my situation, and he said to get into a room he pointed to. I did . . . he came in a few times. When he was done, he showed the new tooth to me. It was perfect. That was his specialty. He charged me $50 and wished me well. I still have that tooth.

Bob Vance, Dick Cutting, and other troops took a Windjammer Cruise on the Yankee Clipper. It was a big sailing ship. We got to take turns at the helm. While Vance was steering, he slowly turned the ship around and when the sailor-in-charge figured that out, we were dismissed. We stopped in great places . . . long before the islands were developed.

Cathie and I went to Hawaii for an AAF Convention. We enjoyed the meetings and got to meet her cousin, who was a psychologist. The next day when we got on a plane to go to Maui, he was sitting on the plane. We never would have known if we hadn't met him the day before. **The first cruise ship Cathie and I took was from LA to Encinada . . . some 3 or 4 days. When I booked it the travel agent said it was $245 for a big room. I thought that was good, until I found out it was per person.

I was offered a trade-out for advertising on a small Greek ship that was going thru the Panama Canal from St. Thomas and arriving in Long Beach. It was a maiden voyage for the ship. We flew to St. Thomas and took the best stateroom available . . . there were only four with bathtubs. I think I paid some cash, but not much.

We met Jay Johnstone (the professional baseball player) and his wife, Mary Jane, who had a suite next to ours. The ship only held 260 people. One night a Pacific storm was so bad that only 5 people showed for dinner . . . Cathie was one who didn't get seasick. The ship had a big reception when we arrived in Long Beach because it was its first time in the US . . . fire hoses and the works. The Duffys, who watched the kids, met us with the kids in Long Beach. It was a neat trip!

On Cathie's 50th birthday we had a party at the Pyrenees. I gave her a book saying we had some good and bad news. The good news was that we were going on a cruise to Mexico with the Ramseys, Browns, Cunninghams, and Lunds. The bad news was that we were going tomorrow! We all did go down to the port in a van. As a surprise I had arranged for her sisters Barb and Claire to join us. They surprised her one at a time and she was really moved. It was a great trip and everyone had fun.

We had another Mexican cruise with our Rotterdam friends, Stu and Henrietta Real. Stu had been in the service with Hugh Bartenstein from Bakersfield, and they joined us. It was a great time hearing them exchange memories.

The big trip for the family was on the Rotterdam in 1978. It was a 17-day Christmas cruise thru the Caribbean, starting and ending in New York City. We had neat dinner companions . . . Henrietta and Stu Real, a retired army Colonel. Lynn (before she was married to Bernie Lebeau) went with us. It was the first ship to get into Cuba after the Crisis and it was an experience. The gals enjoyed the run of the ship. Cathie formed a surprise 50th birthday party for me. I got a hint that something was going on when Stu asked me to have a drink. I told him I couldn't. He told me he was told to do it. That was the "hint". When we left the bar there were "Ed is 50" stickers all over the place, including the elevator where we went to the glass penthouse room and 50 people were there. Cathie told me that they wouldn't let her charge to our account because the accounts were closed . . . we would get to Newport from Havana the next day. She stole a bunch of my American Express checks and paid the bill.

We remember some of the passengers, like Peter and the Wolf, Ditto, the crunch family, etc. It was a great adventure for all concerned. Cathie had figured it was the last time we would all be together. NOT! The kids wanted to know what we were going to do the next Christmas.

We went to the Bahamas and boarded the Canadian American Line. It was a 60-passenger boat that could go places that cruise ships couldn't. It was Meri's 21st birthday the day before we left. We all went to New Orleans from the Bahamas where the kids got to see the French Quarter, eat at Antoines, stay at the Royal Orleans, and see Independence Hall, and then we flew home to reality.

Next year it was Tahiti . . . on Exploration Cruises 60-passenger ship. We saw Bora Bora, Papiette, and other islands. We went to a hotel bar on one of the islands and the Greens, who had been in the Bahamas with us, yelled at us. They were on a freighter for six months and it was in Tahiti for a week. Small World!

The next year we went on a cruise around the Hawaiian Islands. We stopped at an Island every day. It's a great way to see Hawaii. They arrive in port very early in the morning, and leave late at night. On envelope day (for tips) we had gotten a box of 50 cheap Christmas Cards. We all wrote little notes on each one. The gals would put a dollar in one, and say something like . . . this isn't all, there might be more to come. Same with a couple of $5. We put the generous tip in one of them. The box with 50 cards in it was given to our waiter at breakfast, and when we got there for dinner he said that the whole crew was watching him open them. They thought it was great!

We went to Cancun for Christmas one year . . . the Clingers, Hopples, and Sherwoods were there. Cathie's luggage didn't arrive, so we bought a tight bathing suit for her. She was glad when it finally did arrive. On New Years Eve the young ones went out, and Meri's credit card got scammed. During the week we were there they let the Mexican Peso float. You could get a tube of Colgate toothpaste for 19 cents. We had dinner at a very exclusive restaurant. The piano player wore tails! When the American Express bill came it was $78 dollars. It should have been $78 *a person* for four people.

When the Concorde was relatively new Cathie and I took the QE2 to London, saw some shows and came back on the Concorde. It cost us $300 more a person additional, instead of coming back on a 747. Kae Babcock and I did the same thing the ninth day before the Concorde quit, and we each paid $7500 for the airfare. *BIG* difference! (By chance, the Sherwoods were on the QE2 going over).

Cathie and I surprised the Swobodas by joining their cruise around Australia and New Zealand. We liked it, especially liked the people in New Zealand. They went all out for us.

The Lunds, Claire Moeschler (Cathie's sister), Pam Moeschler (Claire's daughter) took the Crystal Harmony around Italy and the Mediterranean. We did Florence, Venice, Pisa, Rome, the Vatican, Monaco, and got off at Barcelona. We stayed at a hotel where some bull fighters were staying. They let us take pictures of them in the hotel. Claire, Pam and the Hopples flew to Paris the next day . . . stayed a couple of days and then flew home. It was an adventure. I think I traded $10G's of it for advertising. It was on the Crystal Harmony at the bridge seminar that I met and sat by chance with Rod Rodriguez who started Palmilla in Cabo. His stories were *really* interesting. I found him to be a very nice, refined, intelligent, classy individual.

In the early 70's six couples hired a yacht . . . The Cantamar. It was a great ship that Sinatra, Earl Schieb and other celebrities had often chartered. Our gang . . . the Hopples, Allens, Uhrans, Lunds, Bades, and Owens had the ship to ourselves. We had great food, good fishing, and lots of fun. Doris slept in Sinatra's bed . . . different times. We boarded in La Paz and seven days afterwards they let us off in Loreto. Susan, Cathie and I went to Loreto for a few days that Christmas Holiday and the Cantamar came in. The Captain let us go on the ship for a drink. He wanted Susan to join him, but she turned it down. It was chartered by some retired firemen. It was a good thing because a few days later we read that it sank in a tremendous storm. No one was lost because the firemen knew how to handle it.

The Swobodas joined us on a cruise thru the inland waterway to Alaska. We then flew to Fairbanks and were entertained by Doris and Dwain Miller. Doris is musical, and Dwain fishes and plays gin. He had retired in Boulder and was moonlighting in Alaska. We then took the train to Denali and stayed in the hotel there. We took a tour on a beautiful day and saw some wonderful wild animals. We then took the special train to Anchorage and had awesome views of Mt. McKinley from the observation car. Paul and I played gin while not observing. We stayed in Anchorage one night and flew back to Vancouver and then home.

While at Underwood the Sheffields, Lunds, and Cathie and I took a seven day New England cruise on the New Shoreham II. It is owned and operated by the Canadian American Line in Warren, Rhode Island. The ship holds about 60 people. It can lower the front and land on any shore. It was the same as the New Shoreham that we had enjoyed in the Bahamas. I guess I was on their mailing list! We hit Block Island, on Long Island NY; Martha's Vineyard; Newport, Rhode Island; Cape Cod, Massachusetts; Nantucket and then we returned to Warren, Rhode Island. It was a simple but interesting trip. Then we all drove back to Underwood.

The Lunds and Swobodas joined us on a trip around South America. We left the day Sid Sheffield died. Doris paged me at the Bakersfield airport and told me the news. Cathie and I were boarding. I told her that Sid would be furious if he knew that we had stayed home. She agreed. Doris and Jack were taking a different airline and left about an hour after we did. We boarded in the port for Santiago, Chile, stopped at a few spots, went around the Horn and were headed for the Falkland Islands. Early birds tendered in, a storm came up and they couldn't get back. The ship sailed up and back waiting for the seas to quiet down. They did but we missed the next port in Argentina.

We got to Montevideo, Uruguay for a short stay and then to Buenos Aires. Even Marsha Swoboda liked the Argentinean beef we had for lunch. We all flew home, having had a wonderful time and celebrated Sid's life with prayer and bourbon.

Don Brown and I took a freighter, The Muskox, from Montreal to Brussels. We were in Underwood when they called and said it would be OK to board. Jim Brandt drove us up, and we climbed aboard. It had 1400 containers and five deep "pits" for grain, etc. We went up the St. Lawrence and stopped to pick up some iron pellets. There were 11 passengers. The staterooms were spacious . . . they used to have a big crew but didn't need one now with modern technology. Don Brown and I would record a report every night on what we did and saw.

On the 4th of July Don and I decided to have a party. All the passengers and crew were invited. We decorated the officers' lounge with toilet paper.

We wore shorts and a blue blazer. They had said they had a duty free-shop on the ship. It was a closet with a bunch of stuff in it. We got a bottle of everything . . . six bottles . . . and it was $31 USD. They all loved it, and we asked the Captain where one of the Officers was. He said that he was running the ship. The Captain then picked up the phone and told him to shut it down and come on up to the party. You could hear the ship wind down. He was there about half an hour and then they decided they had to get going again. You could hear the ship wind back up again and we were on our way.

The other nine passengers were interesting. I won't go into detail, but we put "Harvey" in the 12th sitting place. All had fun with the imaginary Rabbit, brought him food, talked to him, and even brought him presents. After Amsterdam we went to Brussels and disembarked. Don and I took the train to Paris, and flew home the next day. It was a unique adventure.

Cathie and I decided we should ride the Delta Queen. We chose to start in New Orleans, and after some river venues we took the inland waterway to Galveston. We enjoyed Dickens on the Strand, a grand old-time yearly event where sixteen square blocks are decorated and everyone is dressed in clothes of the Charles Dickens era . . . very formal. On the inland waterway they had some fun things, like playing the calliope, flying kites, and waving to people on the shore. The Queen only does the inland waterway once or twice a year, and it's an event for the people to come watch the ship pass. We then bused to Houston and flew home.

The ship is a national treasure . . . still running by act of Congress. The rooms are small. We were warned and had a suite, and it was like a regular hotel room. The jazz musicians aboard were awesome.

In 2003 the Swobodas and Kae and I decided to take the Copper Canyon Rail Trip in mainland Mexico. We flew from Cabo to Los Mochis . . . where Rob Balderrama took care of us royally. He owns a condo at Las Misiones, plus the Baja Surf Hotel and "7 Seas Restaurant" in San Jose. He also owns the bunch of hotels in the Copper Canyon. He had a driver take us to the first hotel about 50 miles from Los Mochis in El Fuente and we stayed at the Pasada Hotel. The next morning we caught the train to Bahulchivo, where a bus met the four of us and took us to the Mission Hotel in Cerocahui. It was a dirt road. The next day they were taking us back to the train and the dirt road was closed. A truck was stuck coming the other direction, so they asked if we would mind riding to the train on it. We said OK, and there we were riding with some hay, tires, barbed wire, our baggage and us. We made the train in time and it was a neat experience . . . especially the people laughing as we entered the town . . . literally tourists on a truck.

The next hotel was a cliffhanger . . . Hotel Mirador at Barrancas. The view was awesome!. The final hotel was up the canyon in Creel . . . the Hotel Sierra Bonita. You passed a zoo to get to the restaurant. Kae broke her ankle on the trail leading to the falls. and they treated her very well. Our tour driver Oscar babied her and helped her on the train, and the conductor let us sit in the dining car all the way back to Los Mochis. Balderrama ran the dining and bar car on the train.

When we got off the train they took us to the hotel. The driver asked for a wheelchair, and they brought one with six casters from the bar. We pushed Kae in it all the way to our room . . . and back the next day to catch our flight back to Cabo. All in all, it was great fun, lots of gin playing, and scenery you could never forget. I recommend it highly . . . and give thanks to Balderrama for making it so comfortable . . . and inexpensive.

In 2007 Steve and Merry McCalley and Kae and I flew to London to see John Farrer's Symphony Conductors Workshop. Only 5 days but we got around . . . saw "Wicked", "Boing Boing" and "Mary Poppins." We returned to Underwood. Great trip with neat travelers!

A number of times our program Director took us to see his friend, Paco, in Culiacan, Mexico. They really turned it on for us. We went interesting places, and Paco had about a dozen men watching out for us so we didn't get roughed up. John Uhran, John Jackovich, Bob Duffy, Rev. Bill Ward (really a bank president), Dave Vordermark (also a bank president), and Trent Jones were some of the travelers.

A unique trip that Cathie and I took was a tour that included 3 days in Kenya, 6 days in the Seychelles Islands (in the Indian Ocean south of Madagascar), and 3 days in Luxor, Egypt. It started in NYC on a chartered configured 767. There were many business class seats. They took us to Manchester, England, gave us a cup of coffee, and then we went to Kenya. We stayed in a camp and saw all the animals in their real habitat. I also took a hot air balloon ride where you could see all kinds of wild animals. We then flew on the same airplane in the same seats to the Seychelles and boarded a Renaissance small ship that only had suites. They passed off the snorkeling beaches as the best in the world, but Cabo's are better. We toured for 6 days and then boarded the same plane to Luxor. It was interesting but Egypt was not our favorite. We then flew home. That plane did the same routine every three days. It was an interesting group of people . . . but all in all we didn't enjoy it so much as other trips we had taken.

The Hopples, Dixie and Dalton Ford, Louise and Bob McCarthy, Judy and Tom Franconi took a private train car from NYC to Sacramento. We started at Underwood, then had a van take us to NYC. We stayed at the Waldorf Astoria on the Junior League Floor. The rooms were so small that we had to drink in the hallway. Others did too, and we met some fine folks.

The next morning we went to Penn Station, where we boarded. We were in a series of three cars . . . one to eat in, one to sleep in, and one that was a "heavy" . . . meaning three axles at each end. The platform was neat, and we waved to lots of people as if we were celebrities. The train went to Washington DC where we had some time and picked up some more private cars. It was then off to Chicago, and our car was still the last car. We did a lot of waving.

We stopped for 10 or 12 hours in Chicago. That's where the trainmaster sorts out the cars. More private cars were added. When we left we were still the last car . . . rearmost is foremost in "training." We stopped in Kansas City . . . added more cars . . . we were still the last car. We went thru Royal Gorge (where passenger trains no longer went); cars and photographers were all along the way. We stopped in Sparks, Nevada, after going thru the great Salt Flats. We finished by going thru the Donner Pass and into Sacramento.

We got to see all the private cars at the stops, and they all had great history . . . famous passengers, first class facilities, and interesting histories. Don Brown met us in a Van in Sacramento and drove us back to Bakersfield. That was *quite* an adventure.

When the kids were young, Frank and Jan Tindle invited the whole gang . . . Hopples, Moeschlers, Clingers, and nanny Brownie . . . to Hilton Head

Island. It was just beginning to catch on, and we had a ball. Seven young kids and a nanny worked the facilities over. For thanks we wrote a poem called "Ode to Papa Boat" (that's what Pam Moeschler called her grandfather Frank). We played golf, saw Harbor Town, ate too well, and even went thru an Easter Egg hunt with a massive bunch of kids. Everyone enjoyed it, especially the individual charge cards to the Plantation Club.

It goes without saying that we ventured to Las Vegas, Pioche, Carpenteria, Lake Tahoe, Buffalo, Laughlin, Nevada, and other venues throughout the years.

We drove the kids East on a six week summer trip. We hit Yellowstone, Deadwood SD, Mount Rushmore and The Bad Lands, and got to my parents' place in Michigan on the ferry. We then went to Buffalo, Underwood, thru Canada to Banff, Lake Louise, down to Seattle and thru California to home in Bakersfield. It was educational for the kids, and I think it widened their knowledge of the United States. It was well worth the time and effort!

Sid Sheffield and I took a trip to Barrow, Alaska, for a bowl of chili. Briefly, it was done on Alaskan airmiles (only 25,000 each); we stayed at the "Top of The World Hotel"; we never saw sunlight; we ate at Pepe's North of the Border. A Tamale, rice and beans, which would be $4.95 tops in Bakersfield, was $23; it was a felony to have a 5th of booze; there were no bars; a special at the one grocery was a dozen donuts for $9.99; there was a tremendous display of non-alcoholic wines; everything from trucks to toothpicks had to be flown in; we toured in a cab the next morning and then caught the plane back to Anchorage. We were warned about polar bears all around, but we never did see one. The sun was rising about 10am as we flew out of Barrow . . . headed for Anchorage, San Francisco, Los Angeles, and Los Cabos. Cathie had gone down to Cabo from Los Angeles as we headed to Barrow. We got there a day after she did. I beat Sid at gin going north. He recouped it all going south! It *was* another adventure for the books!

Phil and Eileen Knowles went with me to Churchill, Manitoba, Canada to see the polar bears. Cathie didn't want to go. We had a cool trip . . . saw a bunch of polar bears in the wild. I think they lock them up and let them out for the tourists. It was a great!

The radio stations created a trip to Costa Rica . . . for clients. In this book is a letter outlining the details. We stayed in town, but took a train trip to the Atlantic Ocean. I remember the kids selling fruit on one stop had a Giumarra Farms (from Bakersfield) grape box to carry the fruit to the train to try to sell. It was in the middle of nowhere.

The classiest trips we took were in the Caribbean on the Whitehawk. It was JD's 104-foot sailboat in the Caribbean. He mentioned to me that we should go play around for a few days on it. I told him I didn't know how to sail. He said we didn't have to . . . it had a crew of five. I said I couldn't afford it, and he asked "how's buying the food and tipping the crew sound?" That got my attention!

Bob and Louise McCarthy, Jack and Doris Lund, and Cathie and I took it for a week. Absolutely fabulous! We left Antigua and toured some islands. They were to let us off on Anguilla, where Barb and Mal Clinger were staying. We had reservations the next day at that resort. We anchored in front, the "staff" took us in and we were told which bungalow the Clingers were in. When we knocked on their door, Barbie said that she thought we were coming tomorrow.

We pointed to the Whitehawk and told her that we were here compliments of JD. She knew JD, and had admired the sailboat but didn't know we were on it. We arranged to have the staff pick them up and bring them out for cocktails and a gourmet dinner. We did same, enjoyed the evening, and shuttled them back to their hotel. The manager of the hotel asked who it was, and Barb told him that it was her sister. He asked how the boat was, and Barb said it was super . . . especially the mahogany bathtub. Barbie said the passengers were coming to his hotel tomorrow for a 4 day stay.

The manager wondered where we were going to be. We paid the same $250 a night but he put us in a suite with its own swimming pool, a living room with three couches and a bottle of booze by each one. The shower was big enough to play bridge in and not get wet if someone took a shower. The view was just magnificent. The Clingers came over to *our* place! We ferried to St Maarten, and flew home after a wonderful trip.

The second trip on the Whitehawk was with Ian and Ruth Falkner, Paul and Marsha Swoboda, and the Hopples. We touched a number of islands and had a great time. Paul and Marsha went with us to British Tortola, where we celebrated Paul's 70th birthday. Debbie and Mike Segrist had a catamaran which we enjoyed; one of the daily trips was to Jost Van Dyke where we saw "Foxy". Believe it or not, Cathie died 5 weeks after that trip. She did get to Denver and Megan Gallagher's wedding a week before she died.

I think this gives a pretty good summary of some of the traveling I/we did. I know I missed a few things, but this overview should give a reader a good insight into our travels through the years. In January, 2009, Kae and I are booked on the QM2 for an 85-day cruise around the world. I hope we make it. That's about it folks! Details of that trip are in the P.S. Chapter.

Books in My Library by People or about Places I have known . . . My library at the office and the one at home have grown over the years. Most of the books are by people I have known, or places I have lived, or about people I have had contact with. I'll put them in capital letters and then add a comment if there is something to say about it. KERN'S MOVERS AND SHAKERS by Camille Gavin. Somehow I'm in the book, and so are many of the people from Kern County that I knew; HELL'S GATE by Dorothy Hayden Truscott. I first met Dorothy when I was 12 at Underwood. She wrote bridge books and was an internationally known bridge expert. I was in her Adirondack camp one time when she was writing on her computer. She told me she was writing a novel about the origin of New York City, and said that writing was her first love. Bridge was her second.

BID BETTER, PLAY BETTER by the same Dorothy Truscott, is a renowned bridge book, revised after twenty years to show the changes in the game . . . what's in and what's out; LOSt CABOS by Bob Jackson relates how the Los Cabos area was born and how it evolved. It is dedicated to Rod Rodriguez, who started Pamilla and is mentioned throughout. This is the same "Rod" that Cathie and I met on the Crystal Harmony cruise around Italy and the Mediterranean.

FROM BLUEBIRDS TO BIG SCREENS by Dave Urner. It's the story of Urner's Appliance store in Bakersfield; THE BEST OF MUKO by Dennis Havens. He also wrote a number of published novels. He was an announcer for us in Las Vegas and Bakersfield, and also was a professional musician. He says he wrote the novels between the first and second shows on the Vegas Strip. THEY TOO WORE PINSTRIPES by Brent Kelley. It's the story of the NY Yankees who were **not** the Joe DiMaggios, Mickey Mantles, Yogi Berras, and other "Stars" of the team. Brother-in-law Rip Coleman is on the cover. AND THE GIRLS SAW EUROPE by Ann Thomson. She was Mom's best old-time friend. It is a vanity book in which my Mother is prominent. After reading it my sister Sal said she now knew who she was.

THE NEW YORK TIMES BRIDGE ENCYCLOPEDIA by Alan Truscott. It was *the* authority when published. Dorothy Truscott's husband, Alan Truscott, was the bridge editor of the New York Times. We enjoyed each other at Underwood.

THE WORLD'S MOST EXTRAORDINARY YACHTS by Bobrow and Jinkins. It has a four-page spread on the Whitehawk, JD's sailboat, described elsewhere in this book. ATLANTIS IN AMERICA BY George Erickson. George has a condo at Misiones and used my computer to write some of this book. His was being fixed. A CLASH OF VALUES by William Mandelaris (Bill Manders). Bill was a Bakersfield TV-Radio announcer and talk show host. I helped him financially to get this book published. At this writing he is on a big station in Reno, Nevada.

THE UNDERWOOD CLUB 1908-1991 by Pat Snyder. It is the story of the Underwood Club and the area around it by Pat Snyder. She was associated with the Club for many years. LIFE WITH A LUSTY PIONEER by A. H. Karpe. He was a legend in early Kern County and built the house we lived in at 2131 Elm Street.

THEY CAME TO BAKER STREET by Reginald Johnson. It is about Sherlock Holmes and Reg was a longtime member of the Underwood Club until his passing; GENEALOGY OF THE LIFE OF CHARLES EVANS HUGHES by Bill Johnson, son of Reg. Bill's wife Brucie is Hughes' granddaughter. They both are at Underwood. MY LIFE AS I CARE TO REMEMBER IT by Ed Brandt Sr., another Underwood member. It is exactly as advertised. DRUGS, SOCIETY, AND HUMAN BEHAVIOR (I have the 9th edition) by Charles Ksir. We've known each other a long time. He is the son-in-law of Jerry Hoos. He's married to Sandy. It is a long-established textbook. He said he does well revising it every year or so.

And then there's WYOMING—A RETROSPECTIVE by Buzz Guckenberger. It is the story of the town of Wyoming, Ohio where I grew up. There are lots of friends and relatives in it, and plenty of nostalgic places. FROM WOOD CHIPS TO GAMBLING CHIPS . . . the story of North and South Lake Tahoe. The Tahoe Biltmore takes a few pages. SHOTGUNS ON SUNDAY by Joseph E. Doctor. It is the story of the wild Bakersfield in the early days. Included is Burt Tibbet, the father of the famous tenor, Lawrence Tibbet. It was republished by the Bakersfield Ad Club for the Kern bi-centennial; GENTLEMAN JOE by Joe O'Brian. He lived in Shafter and was a famous harness driver and horse trainer; WHAT'S A MOUSE (computer illiteracy) and COME DOWN FROM THE POLE, JOEY by Joe Gottlieb in Bakersfield. He ran Seatcover City and advertised with us.

There are some one-of-a-kind bound books like THE GOSPEL ACCORDING TO SAINT SID . . . a collection of the letters and e-mails that Sid Sheffield sent over time to Cathie and me summarizing what happened that week in Bakersfield. HOW TO BUILD A SPANISH LANGUAGE RADIO STATION . . . a collection of Bank of America overdraft slips, dedicated to Everett Murray of the Bank of America who helped us through hard times. Six or seven bound books of the "funny" e-mails I have received through the years. POLITICS, PEOPLE, PHILOSOPHY AND POTPOURRI . . . a couple of bound collections of e-mail and other sources I thought worth saving; MEMORABILIA BOOKS on each of the kids with stuff we had collected thru the years. I gave each one her book for Christmas 2007. There is also a bound book about my Dad and one about me in my library. A DOZEN GENERATIONS . . . about the Hopple heritage. A PHOTO ALBUM done by my mother. It starts with me at birth and has monthly pictures . . . and adds sister Sal for a year or so. It has great pictures, which I had copied and gave to each of the gals. I still have a couple. *Last and least* is PAPAHOPPLE'S PICTURE PARADE—FIRST TRY . . . some 300 pictures with captions of who we were and what we did.

Other Memorabilia . . . I did a piano CD . . . Papahopple Practices (but not enough). Cathie had told me to record some the the piano doodling on tape for the girls. I was actually doing it when someone from Discmakers called . . . thinking I was still in the radio business . . . about a special on CD's. For $595 they would do 100 CD's, with print copy, recorded, and in individual packages. I said why not. Bill Curtis said we had portable digital recording equipment at Disney Radio. He brought it down to the office, we recorded a few tunes and sent them off. When they were about to produce the record I got a call saying I could have all I wanted at twenty five cents a copy. I again said why not . . . and told them to send me a couple of hundred. They took it as $200, and when the order came there were 900 CD's. I still have a *big* bunch.

I did compile all the old 16mm movies, our 8 and super 8mm movies, and some video tapes. The result is that I have a DVD of "Hopples", "Ice Cutting", "Underwood", "Christmas at 2131 Elm", Shell's Wonderful World of Golf in Cabo", the big Cabo Storms and a couple of others. With this book I am through documenting stuff. It's all out there now. The following pages include some certificates etc. Maybe it should be called an appendix, or post script, or plain B. S.

Helpers Past and Present . . . There are plenty of people in my life that have helped me, and I appreciate them all. MARK RAMSEY did the cover for this book; MARY GRAFF edited it for me and got it into the position where we can make any changes before it's published; MIKE ALLEN, who has worked with me for almost 30 years. He and his wife KRISTY are wonderful and lifelong friends; DARLENE TAYLOR, GERRY WELCH, and BARBARA ROONEY, secretaries and helpers; ANN BRAUN, my CPA; JOHN BOWMAN, my barber; JIM KIRKPATRICK, my dentist; BERNIE LEBEAU, my lawyer and his wife, LYNN, who has been a loving friend and helped run the Williams Ranch for us; PATTY ALEXANDER, my nails and toe keeper; IRA COHEN my financial consultant, DR. MARK ABATE, my oncologist; CHARLIE LYNCH and DAVE PARKER, my quasi-promoters; CHASE and VICKI - great cooks and TITO's tipsters; KIM and CARLA ANDREATTA, my friends and rolling stock advisors; DR. WILLIAM GEBHART at the Santa Barbara Clinic who caught my prostate cancer *early*. It's been in remission for 14 or more years; BOB BOVEE . . . friend and political guru; Brother-in-law MAL CLINGER . . . Microsoft tipster; LARRY DENTON, ASHLEY MITCHELL and CORY BRONSON . . . caretakers at the Underwood Club; JORGE DIAZ, who manages Las Misiones in San Jose Del Cabo; MARILYN CURTIS catering; CHARLIE WHITE, the pool man; DOTTIE RAMSEY . . . laugher; Many who have cleaned or helped in the yards for me at various times in various venues . . . JERRI RATLIFF, MARIA ELENA, SYLVIA, CHRISTINE, LINDA VASQUEZ, FLORENTINO JACINTO and TED'S gardening service. Thank you all so much!!!

BARBARA ROONEY, secretary and bookkeeper, was the radio station den mother, and ear to what was going on at the stations. She did the books, guarded the place when I was gone for long vacations, and made life much easier for me; JOYCE DUFFY, a wonderful friend since Las Vegas, wife of BOB DUFFY . . . partner in the radio stations. She is a current savior by coming to the KMAP office weekly, doing the books, and making it easy on me. I can't thank these two enough for what they have meant to me. I love 'em . . . I really mean that!!!

A word about Kae Babcock . . . I can't thank her enough for encouraging me and helping me do the CD, do the picture book, furnish pictures to me for the Underwood plaque, the books, and many picture frames. She was almost *too* supportive in encouraging me to write this book, and I can't thank her enough. She is a fabulous lady, and I love 'er! I'm very lucky to have her at my side . . . and in my life.

Finale . . . It's been fun and a chore to write this book. You should know that my spelling came from very unreliable sources. Know also that the dates, names, and situations have been decorated with poetic license. It's only fair to say that there were some views, news, and askews that were not fit to print, so I didn't! I thank all the "Y"s in the road. Had I not taken them, who knows what my life would have been? It was luck, not skill! I'll take *luck* anytime. I do hope it continues! Thanks for reading and have a good life.

                                                                    E R H

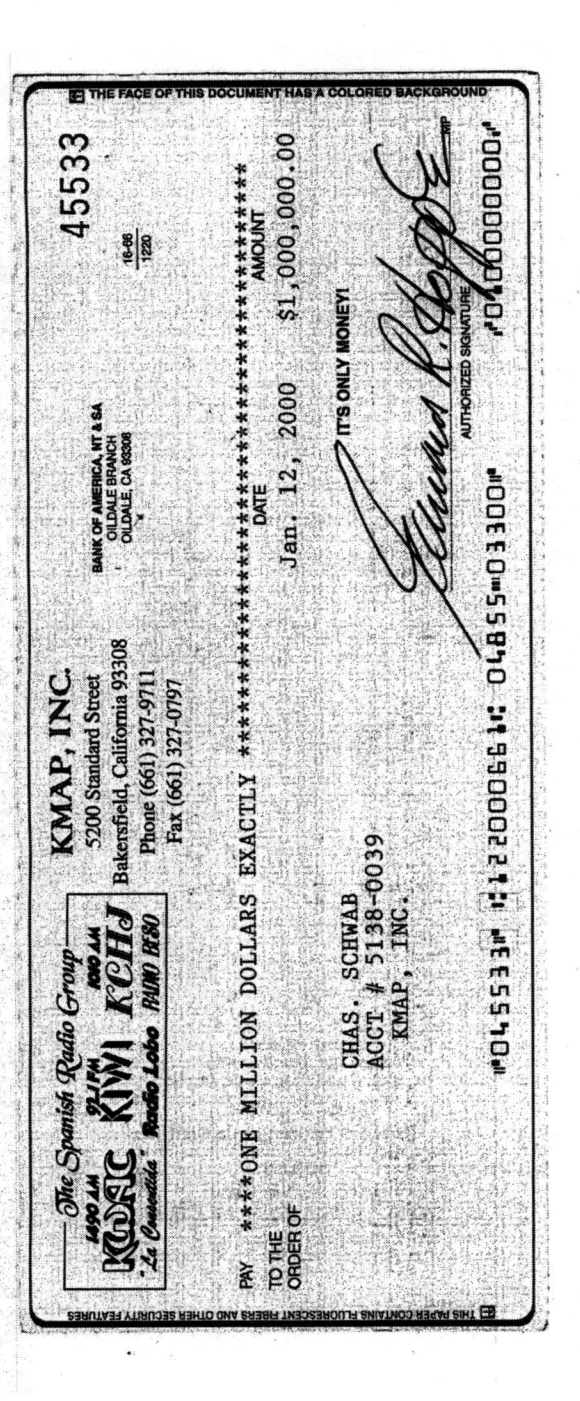

The Only seven digit check I ever wrote.
It ultimately paid the taxes on the stations sale.

ABOUT THE AUTHOR....

(from same . . .)

I was born in Cincinnati in 1930. I really appreciated the parents who had and raised me, instead of someone else. They both had a great sense of humor. I sorta caught a little of that. They said I was a decent kid and didn't cause them much trouble that they knew about. My sister Sal and I went K thru 12 in one building. I was a little above average in high school and college. Along the line I have had a number of working experiences, some of which put change in my pocket and some that took it out. Among them were soda jerk, tour driver, saxophone player, football bookie, bartender, Episcopalian, ad salesman, military stenographer, hotel and casino owner and manager, marketing director, ad manager, skier, guest ranch owner, directorships, trusteeships, vestry member, card player, unicyclist, Republican, college foundation member and chairman, and various radio positions. All that experience taught me very little or nothing to help make a living. I ended up owning and running three Spanish Language radio stations for some 40 years. It was interesting because I didn't know an Ohm from a kilowatt, couldn't run a tape recorder or a broadcast board, and didn't speak Spanish. Why I did well is a mystery to me. It was probably because I had no idea of what I was doing. Good help, good luck, perseverance, perspiration and a supportive (though astonished) wife.

My best accomplishment was getting Cathie to marry me and put up with me. Second was getting and raising the three gals, Lori, Meri and Susan. My third best accomplishment to date is keeping prostate cancer in remission for 14+ years. My Dad said happiness is good health and a poor memory. He was usually right . . . and through life I've found this definition to be better than any I have ever heard.

I hope to spend a few more years in San Jose del Cabo in Baja Sur, at the Underwood Club at Underwood, New York, at Tamarack Pines in Bakersfield, and staying above the grass at all the venues. Cheers!

A BUNCH OF MISCELLANEOUS STUFF THAT I KEPT FOLLOWS.

NONE OF IT IS IMPORTANT, BUT SOMEHOW I FOUND IT INTERESTING. YOUR CHOICE!

The history of the Tahoe Biltmore was difficult to trace because the casino industry, in general, kept a low profile of ownership due to past unsavory characters. This is not to say that any of this property's owners were involved in any wrongdoing.

The story began in 1946, when the Tahoe Biltmore was built by Joseph Blumfeld.

The Tahoe Biltmore later changed its name when Sanford "Sandy" Adler bought it in 1951. Adler, who owned the Can Neva Lodge at the time, renamed the Tahoe Biltmore, the Cal Neva Biltmore.

The Cal Neva Biltmore was sold again to three new owners: David Crow, Eddie Hopple and Jackie Gaughn in 1952. Mr. Gaughn now owns other casino interests in Las Vegas.

In 1956, the Biltmore went through another exciting development, when Joby Lewis built a casino adjacent to the west side of the Cal Neva Biltmore and called it Lewis' Monte Carlo.

In 1958, after 12 years in business, the Cal Neva Biltmore was remodeled and renamed the Nevada Lodge by Meta and Lincoln Fitzgerald. In 1959, the Fitzgeralds purchased Lewis' Monte Carlo and combined it with the Nevada Lodge.

The Fitzgeralds were fascinating owners of the Biltmore. Lincoln Fitzgerald came to Reno in 1946 from Detroit, Michigan. Fitzgerald is credited with being the first individual to put a restaurant in a casino in Reno, Nevada.

Rumors said that Fitzgerald was a former member of the Purple Gang from Detroit. This was never proven, but he was in fact shot twice on the Mount Rose Highway. Interestingly, Fitzgerald requested that the sheriff not investigate his own shootings. To this day, these cases still remain a mystery.

One note of interest is the history of our upstairs convention area, the Nevada Room. Stars like Phyllis Diller (who startled tourists and locals alike with her green hair), Helen O'Connell, Rowan and Martin, and Rudy Vallee, all performed in this room. It didn't stop there—Soupy Sales and Regis Philbin also appeared in the Nevada Room.

In 1985, the Nevada Lodge was purchased by its current owners. In 1986, the Nevada Lodge was changed back to its original name, the Tahoe Biltmore.

Today you sit in the newest addition of the Tahoe Biltmore, overlooking an unforgettable view. With every little change, the Tahoe Biltmore experiences a new beginning to its long-running successful history. We hope this beginning will be a rewarding dining experience. Please come again and thank you for your patronage.

Chuck Cecil's Swingin' Years

18 June 2007

Eddie ...

After messing around with all the enclosed white
pages, I remembered Dave Dexter's PLAYBACK book and
its listing of so many big bands of the swing era.
So, that's (Dexter's book) where I got the list on
the green page. You might want to compare it with
the others. And maybe you don't. And maybe you
should check my speling/typing of the green page!

Good luck with your project and if you need any more
or less information, please give me a call.

Chuck

NOTABLE QUOTE - "It may be hurtful to the pride of statesmen to discover
how little they can really do..to eradicate misery, to alleviate suffering, and improve society. Yet - so it is - the progress of civili-
zation shows more and more how few and simple are the real duties of a
government; and how impossible it is to add to those duties without in-
flicting permanent mischief on a community...But the aim of all statesmen who have acquired a higher reputation has been to remove regulations
and restrictions imposed by others - to remedy the errors of former
statesmen by removing old regulations, and not by imposing new ones.
All that can be said of the great statesman is that he discovered error
and removed it; that he found a country harassed by restrictions and
regulations, and that he freed it."

<u>London Economist</u> <u>1847</u>

	TEAM #1	TEAM #2
SAT 12/20	BUFFALO	GREEN BAY
	ST LOUIS	CAROLINA
SUN 12/21	BALTIMORE	CINCINNATI
	CHICAGO	TAMPA BAY
	INDIANAPOLIS	MINNESOTA
	NEW ORLEANS	KANSAS CITY
	N Y GIANTS	DALLAS
	PHILADELPHIA	WASHINGTON
	PITTSBURGH	HOUSTON
	ATLANTA	ARIZONA
	JACKSONVILLE	OAKLAND
	N Y JETS	DETROIT
	SAN DIEGO	DENVER
	SAN FRANCISCO	SEATTLE
	This is Cathie's Football Pool	
TIEBREAKER	**she played weekly with the**	
	San Jose, CA Police Dept.	
MON 12/22	NEW ENGLAND	MIAMI
	YOUR NAME-	TOTAL POINTS

OPEN DATES: NONE   SUPER BOWL XXXII - SUNDAY JAN 25,1998

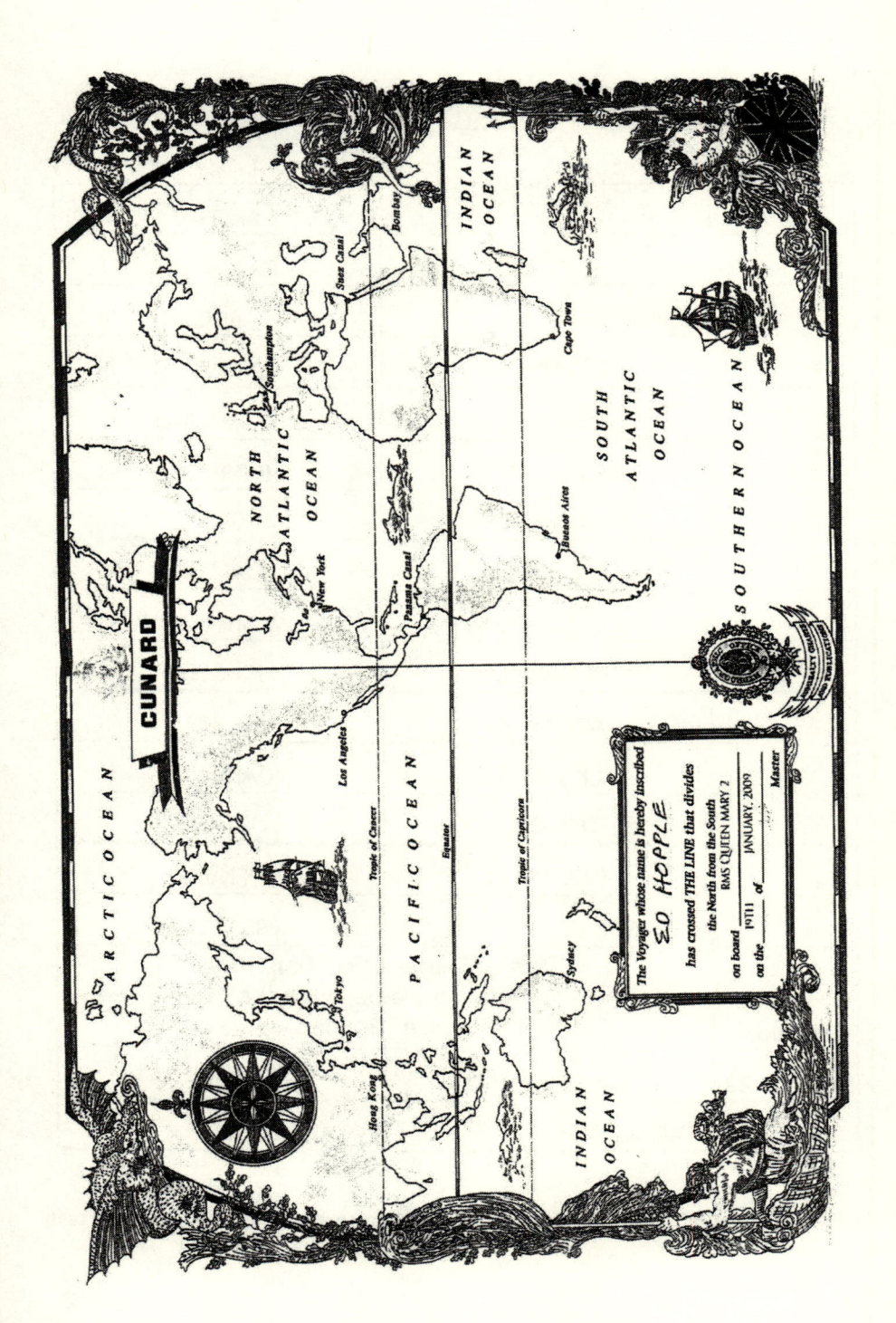

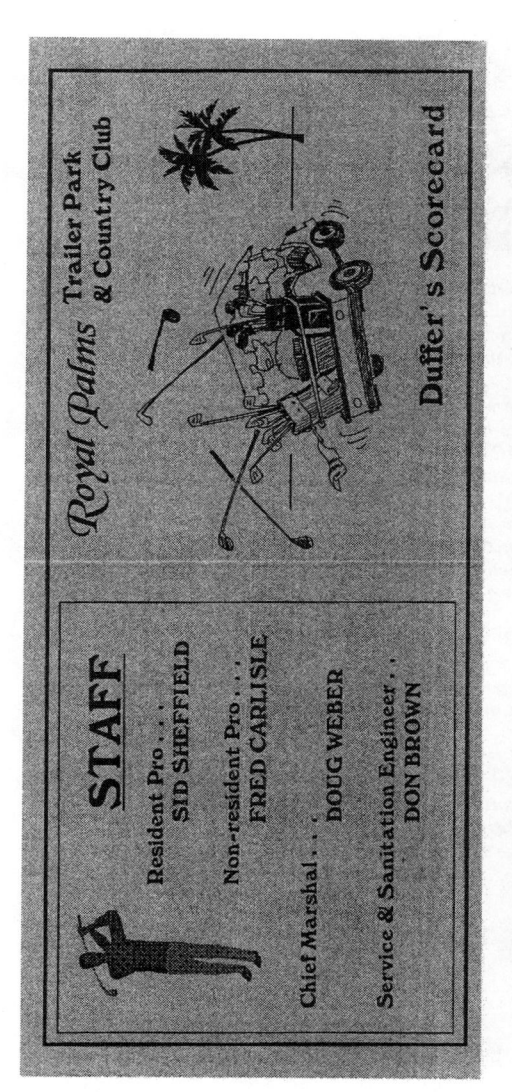

Royal Palms Trailer Park & Country Club

Duffer's Scorecard

STAFF

Resident Pro . . .
SID SHEFFIELD

Non-resident Pro . . . .
FRED CARLISLE

Chief Marshal . . .
DOUG WEBER

Service & Sanitation Engineer . .
DON BROWN

Cleanfax

Person of the 20th Century

Edgar T. 'Ed' York

A man whose contribution is indelibly stamped on the industry he helped to shape

"Good Friends"

There are dozens of parties at this time of year
One over there, and a couple over here
But the one whose renown no one can topple
Is the holiday party thrown by Ed Hopple!

I wait each year with anticipation
For the day I receive the prized invitation
Out to KIWI, KWAC and KCHJ I'll troop
To party with the Spanish Radio Group

With lights and music and food galore
A guest could want for nothing more
From tri-tip to tacos, and even falafel
The only thing missing is a blueberry waffle

But who needs waffles when wine is flowing?
Leaving people merry, with faces glowing
It's a wonderful party, a gala event
Inside the station and outside in tents

So, Mr. Hopple, I send you my thanks
For including me again in your party ranks
Well that's about it; there's no more to tell
So I'll say Merry Christmas!
Wait, make that "No L"!

Marcia Hirst

CHARACTER OF SEPARATION	REPORT OF SEPARATION FROM THE ARMED FORCES OF THE UNITED STATES	DEPARTMENT
HONORABLE		ARMY

SEPARATION DATA

1. LAST NAME — FIRST NAME — MIDDLE NAME	2. SERVICE NUMBER	3. GRADE—RATE—RANK AND DATE OF APPOINTMENT	4. COMPONENT AND BRANCH OR CLASS
HOPPLE EDWARDS RITCHIE	US 52 351 997	SP3(T)23 May 55	AUS

5. QUALIFICATIONS			6. EFFECTIVE DATE OF SEPARATION			7. TYPE OF SEPARATION
SPECIALTY NUMBER OR SYMBOL	RELATED CIVILIAN OCCUPATION AND D. O. T. NUMBER		DAY	MONTH	YEAR	
712.10	Hi		2d	Oct	55	TRFD TO USAR

8. REASON AND AUTHORITY FOR SEPARATION	9. PLACE OF SEPARATION
Rel to USAR AR 635-250 & Sec V SR 615-360-5 SPN 12 I-3	Fort Bragg N C

10. DATE OF BIRTH			11. PLACE OF BIRTH (City and State)	12. DESCRIPTION				
DAY	MONTH	YEAR		SEX	COLOR HAIR	COLOR EYES	HEIGHT	WEIGHT
6	Jan	30	Cincinnati, Ohio	Male	Cau Brown	Blue	5 11"	182

SELECTIVE SERVICE DATA

13. REGISTERED		14. SELECTIVE SERVICE LOCAL BOARD NUMBER (City, County, State)	15. SELECTIVE SERVICE NUMBER	16. INDUCTED		
YES	NO			DAY	MONTH	YEAR
X		#55 Wyoming (Hamilton) Ohio	33 53 30 5	21	Jan	54

17. ENLISTED IN OR TRANSFERRED TO A RESERVE COMPONENT	COMPONENT AND BRANCH OR CLASS	
X	USAR	Trans to USAR (Ohio) Mil Dist.

18. MEANS OF ENTRY OTHER THAN BY INDUCTION				19. GRADE—RATE OR RANK AT TIME OF ENTRY INTO ACTIVE SERVICE
☐ ENLISTED	☐ REENLISTED	☐ COMMISSIONED NA	☐ CALLED FROM INACTIVE DUTY	Pvt-1

19a. DATE AND PLACE OF ENTRY INTO ACTIVE SERVICE			20. HOME ADDRESS AT TIME OF ENTRY INTO ACTIVE SERVICE (No., R.F.D., City, County and State)
DAY	MONTH	YEAR	Place (City and State)	
21	Jan	54	Cincinnati, Ohio	40 Linden Drive, Wyoming (Hamilton) Ohio

SERVICE DATA

STATEMENT OF SERVICE FOR PAY PURPOSES	A. YEARS	B. MONTHS	C. DAYS	20a. ENLISTMENT ALLOWANCE PAID ON EXTENSION OF ENLISTMENT, IF ANY			
				DAY	MONTH	YEAR	AMOUNT
21. NET SERVICE COMPLETED FOR PAY PURPOSES EXCLUDING THIS PERIOD						NA	
22. NET SERVICE COMPLETED FOR PAY PURPOSES THIS PERIOD	1	9	8				
23. OTHER SERVICE (Act of 16 June 1942 as amended) COMPLETED FOR PAY PURPOSES	0	0	0	23a. FOREIGN AND/OR SEA SERVICE			
24. TOTAL NET SERVICE COMPLETED FOR PAY PURPOSES	1	9	8	YEARS 0	MONTHS 0	DAYS 0	

26. DECORATIONS, MEDALS, BADGES, COMMENDATIONS, CITATIONS AND CAMPAIGN RIBBONS AWARDED OR AUTHORIZED
National Defense Service Medal

28. MOST SIGNIFICANT DUTY ASSIGNMENT	29. WOUNDS RECEIVED AS A RESULT OF ACTION WITH ENEMY FORCES (Place and date, if known)
Hq Det XVIII Abn Corps	None

30. SERVICE SCHOOLS OR COLLEGES, COLLEGE TRAINING COURSES AND/OR POST-GRAD. COURSES SUCCESSFULLY COMPLETED	DATES (From-To)	MAJOR COURSES	31. SERVICE TRAINING COURSES SUCCESSFULLY COMPLETED
3d Armd Div Sch, Ft Knox, Ky.	1954	Basic Army Admin	Basic Military Training
AG Sch, Ft Benjamin Harrison	1954	Steno	

INSURANCE AND PAY DATA

32. KIND & AMT. OF INSURANCE & MTHLY. PREMIUM	32a. ACTIVE SERVICE PRIOR TO 28 APRIL 1951			33. MONTH ALLOTMENT DISCONTINUED	34. MONTH NEXT PREMIUM DUE
None Indemnity	☐ YES ☐ NO ☐ UNKNOWN			NA	Feb 56

35. TOTAL PAYMENT DUE OR PAID	36. TRAVEL OR MILEAGE ALLOWANCE INCLUDED IN TOTAL PAYMENT	37. DISBURSING OFFICER'S NAME AND SYMBOL NUMBER
NA	NA	NA

AUTHENTICATION

38. REMARKS (Continue on reverse)	39. SIGNATURE OF OFFICER AUTHORIZED TO SIGN
Blood Group "O" AFQT 100 No days lost under section 6(a) Appendix 2b MCM 1951 Item 3: Pvt-2 (P) 21 May 54 Item 5: Steno Item 8: Trans to USAR for comp of 8yrs under UMTS Act. Entitled to $200.00 MOP. Paid $100.00 on final pay.	*[signature]* NAME, GRADE AND TITLE (Typed) CECIL PITTMAN CWO USA ACTG ASST ADJ GEN

PERSONAL DATA

40. V. A. BENEFITS PREVIOUSLY APPLIED FOR (Specify type)		
COMPENSATION, PENSION, INSURANCE BENEFITS, ETC.		CLAIM NUMBER
None		NA

41. DATES OF LAST CIVILIAN EMPLOYMENT		42. MAJOR CIVILIAN OCCUPATION	43. NAME AND ADDRESS OF LAST CIVILIAN EMPLOYER
FROM	TO	(Coporation)	
NA	NA	President	Eastern States Radio Corp. Columbus, Ohio

44. UNITED STATES CITIZEN	45. MARITAL STATUS	46. NON-SERVICE EDUCATION (Years successfully completed)				MAJOR COURSE OR FIELD
☒ YES ☐ NO	Married	GRAM-MAR	HIGH SCHOOL	COL-LEGE	DEGREE(S)	
		8	4	5	B.A.	Economics

47. PERMANENT ADDRESS FOR MAILING PURPOSES AFTER SEPARATION (St., R.F.D., City, County and State)	48. SIGNATURE OF PERSON BEING SEPARATED
40 Linden Drive, Cincinnati 15 (Hamilton) Ohio	*[signature] Edward R. Hopple*

DD FORM 214 1 JUL 52   EDITION OF 1 JAN 50 IS OBSOLETE   INDIVIDUAL'S COPY (TO BE DELIVERED TO THE INDIVIDUAL BEING SEPARATED)   1

From: Bach
To: Beethoven
And Bach Again!

Merry
Christmas
Bakersfield...

KIWI-FM Stereo 92.1 is pleased to present to Bakersfield a 24-hour Classical Music Station. It's our lasting Christmas gift to Kern County. Classical Music is something we have asked Santa for, and something we can really use. DO NOT OPEN UNTIL CHRISTMAS (Although you might be able to peek a little earlier). As we send this card, we are not absolutely sure of the exact day we will have it gift wrapped and on the tree. . .but it is yours to enjoy, Bakersfield.
Happy Holidays!

CLASSICAL 92
KIWI ♪ FM

Your stereo concert hall • Classical music 24 hours a day

JUDGE JACK E. LUND

INVITES YOU TO BE HIS GUEST AT A

HOT DOG RETIREMENT PARTY

For
"CHIPS"
of WKMC

FREE HOT DOGS - CHIPS - SODA POP

Tuesday, November 22nd
11:30 AM to 1:30 PM

Southside (Rear) of Criminal Justice Building
1215 Truxtun Avenue

MUSIC - FUN - LAUGHTER

TO BE FILLED IN BY COLLECTOR.

Form 1040.

TO BE FILLED IN BY INTERNAL REVENUE BUREAU.

List No. ....

File No. ....

INCOME TAX.

.... District of ....

THE PENALTY
FOR FAILURE TO HAVE THIS RETURN IN
THE HANDS OF THE COLLECTOR OF
INTERNAL REVENUE ON OR BEFORE
MARCH 1 IS $20 TO $1,000.
(SEE INSTRUCTIONS ON PAGE 4.)

Assessment List ....

Date received ....

Page .... Line ....

UNITED STATES INTERNAL REVENUE.

RETURN OF ANNUAL NET INCOME OF INDIVIDUALS.
(As provided by Act of Congress, approved October 3, 1913.)

RETURN OF NET INCOME RECEIVED OR ACCRUED DURING THE YEAR ENDED DECEMBER 31, 191....
(FOR THE YEAR 1913, FROM MARCH 1. TO DECEMBER 31.)

Filed by (or for) .... of ....
(Full name of individual.)   (Street and No.)

In the City, Town, or Post Office of .... State of ....
(Fill in pages 2 and 3 before making entries below.)

1. GROSS INCOME (see page 2, line 12) .... $

2. GENERAL DEDUCTIONS (see page 3, line 7) .... $

3. NET INCOME .... $

Deductions and exemptions allowed in computing income subject to the normal tax of 1 per cent.

4. Dividends and net earnings received or accrued, of corporations, etc., subject to like tax. (See page 2, line 11) .... $

5. Amount of income on which the normal tax has been deducted and withheld at the source. (See page 2, line 9, column A)..

6. Specific exemption of $3,000 or $4,000, as the case may be. (See Instructions 3 and 19)

Total deductions and exemptions. (Items 4, 5, and 6) .... $

7. TAXABLE INCOME on which the normal tax of 1 per cent is to be calculated. (See Instruction 3). $

8. When the net income shown above on line 3 exceeds $20,000, the additional tax thereon must be calculated as per schedule below:

					INCOME.	TAX.
1 per cent on amount over $20,000 and not exceeding $50,000....					$	$
2	"	"	50,000	"	" 75,000....	
3	"	"	75,000	"	" 100,000....	
4	"	"	100,000	"	" 250,000....	
5	"	"	250,000	"	" 500,000....	
6	"	"	500,000			

Total additional or super tax .... $

Total normal tax (1 per cent of amount entered on line 7).... $

Total tax liability.. $

FROM   MY   DAD !!

178

FROM CHUCK CECIL's SWINGIN' YEARS -- Syndicated radio pgm. BIG BANDS of the 1930-1950 era.

Aaronson, Irving
Alexander, Van
Allen, Barclay
Ambrose, Bert
Anthony, Ray
Arcaraz, Luis
Armstrong, Louis
Arnaz, Desi
Arnheim, Gus
Auld, Georgie
Ayres, Mitchell
Ballew, Smith
Barnet, Charlie
Barron, Blue
Basie, Count
Beneke, Tex
Berigan, Bunny
Bernie, Ben
Bestor, Don
Bloch, Ray

Block, Bert
Bostic, Earl
Bradley, Will
Bradshaw, Tiny
Brandwynne, Nat
Breeze, Lou
Brigode, Ace
Bring, Lou
Brooks, Randy
Brown, Les
Burke, Sonny
Busse, Henry
Butterfield, Billy
Byrne, Bobby
Calloway, Cab
Carle, Frankie
Carpenter, Ike
Carter, Benny
Cavallaro, Carmen
Chester, Bob
Clinton, Larry
Coakley, Tom
Condon, Eddie
Cooley, Spade
Coon-Sanders
Cooper, Al
Courtney, Del
Craig, Francis
Crosby, Bob
Crosby, Bob
Cugat, Xavier
Daily, Pete
Davis, Johnny
Davis, Meyer
DeLange, Eddie
Derwin, Hal
Deutsch, Emory
Donahue, Al
Donahue, Sam
Dorsey Brothers

Dorsley, Jimmy
Dorsey, Tommy
Duchin, Eddy
Dunham, Sonny
Ellington, Duke
Elgart Brothers
Elgart, Larry
Elgart, Les
Ennis, Skinnay
Fields, Herbie
Fields, Shep
Fina, Jack
Fio Rito, Ted
Flanagan, Ralph
Foster, Chuck
Fotine, Larry
Fox, Roy
Funk, Larry
Garber, Jan
Gill, Emerson
Gluskin, Lud
Goldkette, Jean
Goodman, Benny
Gordon, Gray
Gray, Glen
Gray, Jerry
Green, Johnny
Geen, Larry
Grier, Jimmy
Hackett, Bobby
Hall, George
Hallett, Mal
Hamilton, George
Hamp, Johnny
Hampton, Lionel
Harris, Phil
Hawkins, Erskine
Hayes, Edgar
Haymes, Joe
Hayton, Lennie
Heath, Ted
Heidt, Horace
Hefti, Neal
Henderson, Fletcher
Henderson, Horace
Henderson, Skitch
Herbeck, Ray
Herman, Woody
Heywood, Eddie
Hickman, Art
Hill, Tony
Himber, Richard
Hines, Earl
Hite, Les
Hoff, Carl
Hopkins, Claude
Horlick, Harry
Howard, Eddy
Hudson, Dean
Hudson, Will
Hudson-DeLange
Hunt, Pee Wee
Hutton, Ina Ray

James, Harry
Jarrett, Art
Jenkins, Gordon
Jenney, Jack
Jerome, Henry
Jones, Isham
Jones, Spike
Jordan, Louis
Jurgens, Dick
Kardos, Gene
Kassel, Art
Kavelin, Al
Kaye, Sammy
Kemp, Hal
Kenton, Stan
King, Henry
King, Wayne
Kirby, John
Kirk, Andy
Knapp, Orville
Krupa, Gene
Kyser, Kay
Lawrence, Elliot
Leonard, Harlan
Lewis, Ted
Light, Enoch
Little, Little Jack
Lombardo, Guy
Long, Johnny
Lopez, Vincent
Lunceford, Jimmie
Lyman, Abe
Madriguera, Enric
Malneck, Matty
Manone, Wingy
Maltby, Richard
Mantovani
Martin, Freddy
Marterie, Ralph
Masters, Frankie
May, Billy
McCoy, Clyde
McFarland Twins
McKinley, Ray
McKinney's Cotton Pickers
McShann, Jay
Messner, Johnny
Miller, Glenn
Millinder, Lucky
Molina, Carlos
Monroe, Vaughn
Mooney, Art
Morgan, Russ
Morrow, Buddy
Moten, Bennie
Nagel, Freddy
Neighbors, Paul
Nelson, Ozzie
Nichols, Red
Noble, Ray
Norvo, Red
Noone, Jimmy
Olsen, George

Oliver, King
Oliver, Sy
Osborne, Will
Owens, Harry
Pastor, Tony
Paxton, George
Pearl, Ray
Pendarvis, Paul
Phillips, Teddy
Pollack, Ben
Powell, Teddy
Prado, Prez
Prima, Louis
Raeburn, Boyd
Ravazza, Carl
Redman, Don
Reichman, Joe
Reisman, Leo
Renard, Jacques
Reser, Harry
Rey, Alvino
Riley-Farley
Rogers, Buddy
Rose, David
Roy, Harry
Sanders, Joe
Savitt, Jan
Sauter-Finegan
Scott, Raymond
Senter, Boyd
Shaw, Artie
Sherwood, Bobby
Shilkret, Nat
Sissle, Noble
Slack, Freddie
Smith, Stuff
Sosnick, Harry
Specht, Paul
Spitalny, Phil
Spanier, Muggsy
Spivak, Charlie
Stabile, Dick
Steele, Blue
Stone, Lew
Strong, Benny
Sullivan, Joe
Teagarden, Jack
Thornhill, Claude
Trace, Al
Tremaine, Paul
Trumbauer, Frankie
Tucker, Orrin
Tucker, Tommy
Vallee, Rudy
Van, Garwood
Ventura, Charlie
Wald, Jerry
Webb, Chick
Weeks, Anson
Weeks, Randy
Weems, Ted
Welk, Lawrence
Whiteman, Paul
Williams, Cootie
Williams, Griff

Dare

"Far better it is to dare mighty things,
to win glorious triumphs,
even though checkered with failure,
than to take rank with those poor spirits
who neither enjoy much nor suffer much,
because they live in the grey twilight
that knows not victory nor defeat."

Be Fabulous

This is to certify that the flag presented with this certificate was flown over the Capitol of the United States especially for presentation to

Mr. Edwards R. Hopple

Member of Congress

DATE FLOWN 11/24/72

CUNARD

In Commemoration of the
Farewell Transatlantic Season of

QUEEN ELIZABETH 2

Cunard Line hereby commemorates this historic Transatlantic Crossing aboard the legendary QUEEN ELIZABETH 2.

After thirty-four years of offering service between New York and Southampton, 2003 marks the

Final Transatlantic Season of the most famous ocean liner in the world.

Edwards Hopple

Ian McTaggart
CAPTAIN

THE MOST FAMOUS OCEAN LINERS IN THE WORLD

Lives remembered

Wm. Hopple ran Stearns & Foster

Street was named after family

By Rebecca Goodman
Enquirer staff writer

HYDE PARK – William Andrew Hopple III, former president of Stearns & Foster, died Saturday at Deupree Terrace in Hyde Park. Mr. Hopple, 102, was the oldest living graduate of Wyoming High School and Kenyon College.

A descendant of a Cincinnati family for whom Hopple Street is named, Mr. Hopple was a "wonderful gentleman, possessing a quick, dry wit and beloved by all," said his nephew, William Anderson of Wyoming.

Mr. Hopple

At 102, Mr. Hopple possessed a tremendous recall, and talked about swimming in the Mill Creek as a teenager, walking to work at Stearns & Foster in Lockland and lighting newspapers to signal the train to Cincinnati to stop for passengers.

Mr. Hopple graduated from Wyoming High in 1920 and Kenyon in 1924. He served 46 years with Stearns & Foster, retiring in 1962. He was also head of the Dominion Wadding Co. in Montreal, and a director of Fifth Third Bank.

He was a member of the Presbyterian Church of Wyoming, where he served a term as chairman of the board. He was also a member of the Wyoming Golf Club and the Underwood Club of New York.

Mr. Hopple was preceded in death by his wives, Mary Ritchie in 1954 and Janet Meyers in 1999, and a daughter, Sarah Hopple Coleman, in 1999.

Survivors include his son, Edwards R. Hopple of Bakersfield, Calif.; four grandchildren; and four great-grandchildren.

A graveside service is 11 a.m. Friday at Spring Grove Cemetery.

Memorials: Wyoming High School Foundation, 420 Springfield Pike, Wyoming, OH 45215 or Kenyon College, Development Office, Gambier, OH 43022-9623.

E-mail rgoodman@enquirer.com

183

Edwards R. Hopple

Alumnis anni MCMLII
ad Almam Matrem hodie revertentibus
per quinquaginta annos semper fidelibus
bellorum multorum et gloriosorum victoribus,
nunc sociis honoris causa
ex animo gratulantur
Collegii Amherstiensis praeses et curatores

a.d. Kal. Iun., MMII

Tom Gerety

PRAESES

Kern's Movers & Shakers

Hopple, Edwards — When Ed Hopple, with his partner, Gordon Sherwood, established KWAC in 1963, it was Kern County's first Spanish language station and one of about eight in California. As Hopple puts it, "We sort of Daniel Boone'd it."

Initially, the station was Spanish for half of its broadcast day and black programming for the remainder. (Maria Elena, Carlos Zapiain and Esteban Lopez-Sierra, all of whom previously had shows on other local stations, were among the first on-air people hired.) The reason half the programming was in English is that advertisers felt there was no "Spanish" market. They soon learned they were wrong and KWAC has become enormously successful.

The station also was a pioneer in convincing entities such as the California Highway Patrol and the American Heart Association they should produce public service announcements in Spanish.

In February 1986, Hopple, Sherwood and Robert Duffy launched another new venture, KIWI-FM, the county's first classical music station.

Each Christmas, Hopple and his wife, Catherine, provide Bakersfield residents with a spectacular display of colored lights and moving figures in the frontyard and on the roof of their two-story home.

Kane, Walter — Walter Kane, who was hired by *The Californian* in 1922 as a $25-a-week advertising sales-

NAT'L ASSOC. OF BROADCASTERS

HARVARD GRAD BIZ SCHOOL

7-16-21-1967

This Certificate is Presented to

ED HOWLE

by the

BETTER BUSINESS BUREAU

in Recognition of

OUTSTANDING SERVICE AS DIRECTOR

1970 - 1982

JANUARY 26, 1982

Oscar Chavez, President

Terry Hilliard, Exec. V. Pres.

MEMBER

National Panel of Consumer Arbitrators

This is to Certify that:

Ed Hopple

Is qualified and has volunteered to serve as an arbitrator in disputes
between businesses and their customers, pursuant to the rules of
THE BETTER BUSINESS BUREAU OF SOUTH CENTRAL CALIFORNIA, INC.

Radio station party 'best in town'

Out and about

denise

CUTBIRTH

The KWAC/KIWI/KCHJ Holiday Party, better known as the "Hopple Party" after radio station owner Ed Hopple, was held again this season. Ed and his wife, Cathie, have been hosting the party for 28 years.

This year the party was held at the radio station, off Pierce Road. Ten-thousand square feet of tent was erected and hundreds of yards of indoor/outdoor carpet was laid. There were six caterers and valet parking to serve the 1,000 who attended, including John Bowman, who boasted he has been Ed's barber for the past 38 years. CSUB professor Judith Pratt came because of the reputation of the party. "I heard it's the best in town," she said. Sabine Westmoreland attended dressed in pewter leather. Others who attended were Frank and Marie Amestoy; Marvin Chesler; Pam and Digger Helm, Rick Ryan and the Hopples' daughter, Merl Roberts, with husband, Steve.

Recording artists Bolero Soul, the internationally famous classical guitarist duet from Guadalahara, Mexico, entertained the dance crowd along with the local band First Echo.

Julie Salazar of Stockdale Argos Travel let out a robust howl or "grito," announcing her delight as "La Bamba" began playing.

"People are going crazy. Look at the dance floor; it's jammed," said Mike Allen, radio station vice president and general manager. Allen's wife, Kristy, was nearby, along with Katy and Tom Hartnett.

Under the tent were a variety of Christmas trees, including one tall flocked tree and one made of green balloons. Food stations were set up throughout the tent, and a score of bartenders quickly tended to guests.

Fike's catered salmon and calamari, Cope's brought tri-tip sandwiches, and Garcia's had a spread of Mexican foods. The baked goods came from Xochil Bakery.

Among those attending were Dr. Mel Cochran and his wife, June, Joyce and Bob Duffy, Dennis and Luanne Kay, Pete Parra, executive director of Employers Training Resource; Juan and Nery Ornales, owners of La Bonita Tortillas; Pete Castro of W.A. Thompson and his wife, Delores; Joe Cornejo of Advanced Beverage and attorneys Daniel and Sylvia Rodriguez.

CALLINE 322-1717

A service of the Bakersfield Californian

To suggest story ideas for Out and About columnist Denise Cutbirth, call 322-1717 and select category 2721. Leave your suggestion, name and a daytime phone number. Or write to her c/o *The Bakersfield Californian*, P.O. Bin 440, Bakersfield, Ca 93302.

WYOMING SCHOOL
FOUNDATION

CERTIFICATE of APPRECIATION

This certifies your Giving Circle and the inscription engraved on the Donor and Volunteer Recognition Walls in the Lobby of The Pendery Center for the Arts at Wyoming High School. This certificate is given with sincere appreciation for your commitment and generosity to preserve the standard of excellence of Wyoming City Schools.

Heritage Circle:
$10,000 - $99,999

Ed Hopple '48
In Memory of Cathie Hopple

Presented at the Celebration and Dedication on September 24, 2002.

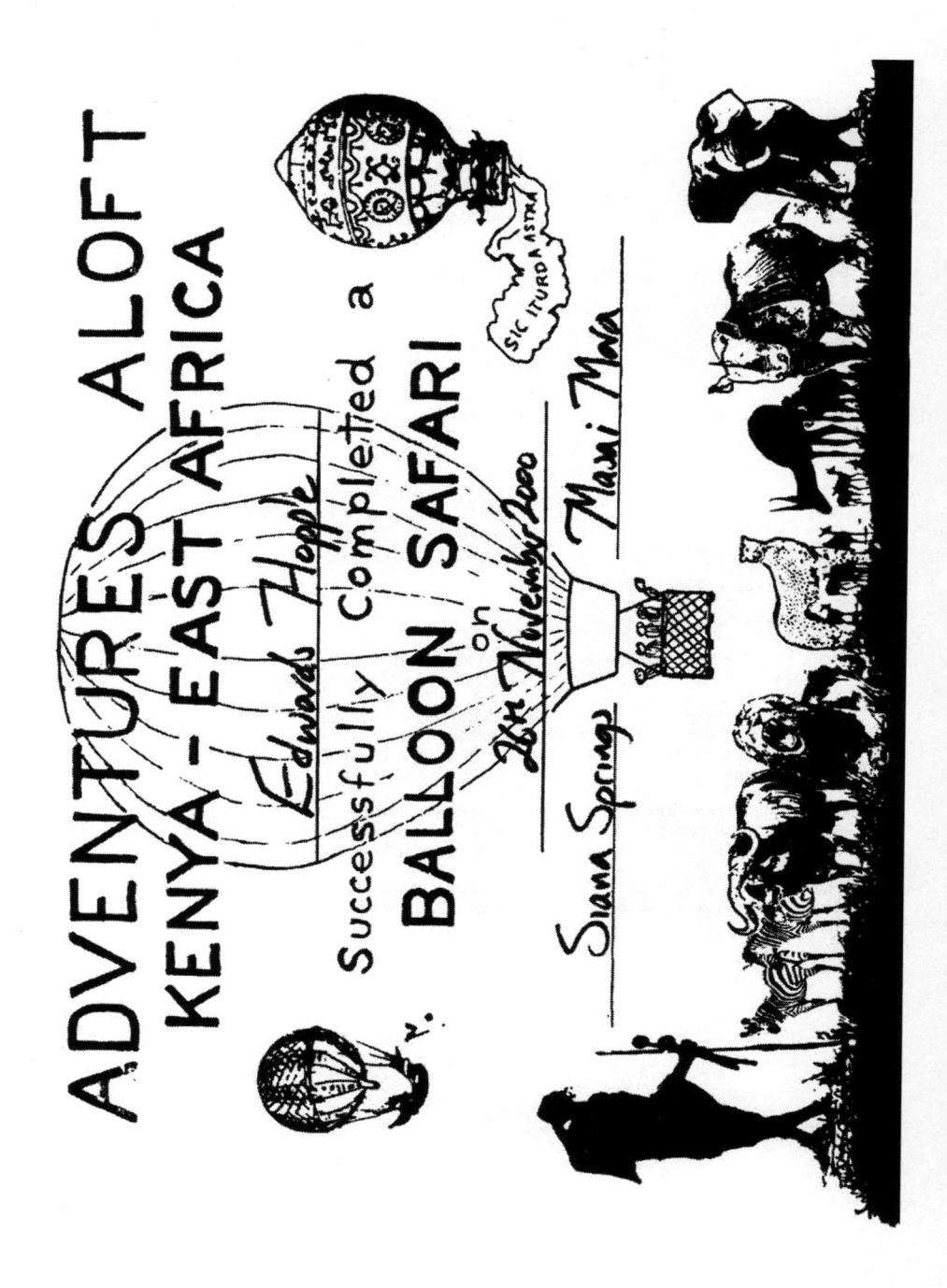

WILLIAM M. KETCHUM
38TH DISTRICT, CALIFORNIA

413 CANNON HOUSE OFFICE BUILDING
WASHINGTON, D.C. 20515
(202) 225-2915

ADMINISTRATIVE ASSISTANT
CHRISTOPHER C. SEEGER

DISTRICT REPRESENTATIVE
DALE J. SILVA

Congress of the United States
House of Representatives
Washington, D.C. 20515

KERN, KINGS, SAN LUIS OBISPO AND
SANTA BARBARA COUNTIES

DISTRICT OFFICES:

800 TRUXTUN AVENUE, #302
BAKERSFIELD, CALIFORNIA 93301
(805) 323-8322

1155 MARSH STREET
SAN LUIS OBISPO, CALIFORNIA 93401
(805) 549-3391

321 NORTH DOUTY, #8
HANFORD, CALIFORNIA 93230
(209) 582-1706

3276 HOLLISTER AVENUE
WING 3, SUITE E
SANTA BARBARA, CALIFORNIA 93111
(805) 964-3514

November 28, 1973

Mr. and Mrs. Edward R. Hopple
2131 Elm Street
Bakersfield, Calif.   93301

Dear Ed and Mrs. Hopple:

Thank you for your response to my questionnaire and for your additional comments relative to welfare recipients and welfare cheaters.

There is simply no excuse for people who won't work receiving public money for their support. Nor is there an excuse for the type of bureaucratic jungle that allows the same person to file for and receive money under different names. The huge apparatus must be brought under control.

I know that there are truly needy people who deserve our help and support. I am committed to their relief. But the drains on our tax money who will not go out and get a job should be cut off at once.

Thank you for your expression of opinion. Please continue to keep me informed of your views on matters of mutual concern.

Sincerely,

WILLIAM M. KETCHUM
Member of Congress

WMK:ls

192

WILLIAM M. THOMAS
MEMBER OF CONGRESS
CALIFORNIA
805-322-2225

May 22, 1990

Mr. and Mrs. Ed Hopple
2131 Elm Street
Bakersfield, CA, 93301

Dear Ed and Cathie,

Thank you for your generous contribution to my campaign fundraiser with the Secretary of Commerce and Mrs. Mosbacher. We had a wonderful event with 700 supporters, and Sharon and I appreciate your help as a Sponsor in ensuring the success of the evening.

I also appreciate knowing that you continue to support my efforts as your Congressman -- in Washington, in the district, and in my goal of securing a Republican majority in the Legislature and the Congress so that we can someday provide the kind of leadership in government that we both want to realize.

Thanks again for your financial support of my campaign.

Warm regards,

Bill

BILL THOMAS

CONTRIBUTIONS TO THIS COMMITTEE ARE NOT DEDUCTIBLE FOR FEDERAL INCOME TAX PURPOSES.

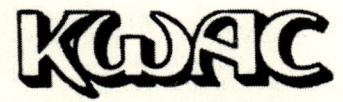

RADIO STATION KWAC • 5200 Standard Street • Bakersfield, California 93308 • Phone (805) 327-9711 • "1490 ON YOUR AM DIAL"

COSTA RICA TRIP

Well, that SPECIAL TRIP is almost upon us. I thought you might like to know a few things about this trip and who will be going. This is the first time we've done a Costa Rica trip so you're pioneering along with us...so anything can happen. Because of this, we're giving you the "scoop" as we know it. We are enclosing the Waiver which we ask you to sign now and return to us in the enclosed envelope...(you're just signing your life away, so don't worry about it...Just sign it!) NO WAIVER...NO TICKEEEE!

1) We depart LAX Friday, March 22nd, at 1:40 AM (that's early early morning) from the LACSA Terminal. NOTE: Please be there approximately 1-1/2 hours prior to departure——this airline in particular overbooks, so don't be one of those who doesn't get on the flight, as there is nothing we can do about it, because these tickets are "exchange" and not re-usable on another airline and are not refundable so we must be there early (midnight Thursday night) Departure: Flight No. 647.

2) We arrive in San Jose, Costa Rica, around 11:40 AM, local time.

3) We will return Tuesday, March 26th, arriving at LAX around 10:30 PM. Arrival: Flight No. 644.

4) Clothes: the temperature is 70°-80° daytime and 50°-60° nights. Very tropical. It is our understanding that they are formal in the Casino at night, so coat and tie for you fellows and the gals should take along dresses in case they do not allow pantsuits in the Casino at night...(like we said, we haven't been there, so it's best to be prepared!)

5) We will be staying at the HOTEL HERRADURA, CUIDAD CARIARI/SAN JOSE, COSTA RICA Telephone: (506) 39-00-33 Telex: 7512 HERRATEL

This Hotel features an 18-hole golf course; 10 tennis courts; gyn; suana; casino and more...see enclosed brochure. The rooms are $44/double per night...plus tax. You are responsible for your room, food, beverage and whatever other expenses you might incur. KWAC takes care of the airfare and that good KWAC Hospitality.

6) VERY IMPORTANT! YOU MUST HAVE YOUR CURRENT PASSPORT with you at LACSA Terminal. If you do not have one, call KWAC at 327-9711 and we will give you some details for applying. You should apply RIGHT NOW and have it marked "RUSH" so you will receive it in time.

7) Those people going on the trip are: Ralph & Gertrude Prejean and Robert & Marily Shaffer of Greenlawn; Jack & Judy Waters of Crosstown Liquors; Louie & Phyllis Hicks of Happy Steak; Paul & Georgia Sisemore of Oak Street Carwash; Sandy & Brenda Chaddick of Fat T's Pizzaeasy; Sid Sheffield of Cal State Bakersfield; Dick & Chrissy Dahlgren of Postal Instant Press; Ed Hopple, Mike Allen and Ramon Garza of Radio KWAC.

We are enclosing two copies of this letter so you may leave one at home in case of an emergency so you can be called. If our staff can be of assistance, please call the office at 327-9711.

Looking forward to a G R E A T   T R I P !!!

Mike allen

Mike Allen
RADIO STATION KWAC

MA:gw
2/18/85

194

Proclamation
Office of the Mayor

The Mayor
of the City of Bakersfield,
California
has officially proclaimed

February 18, 2004

as

Aspiring Tycoons and Toastmasters Day

in our city
in recognition of their 10th anniversary celebration;
in recognition of their unswerving devotion
to the creed, "No service to anyone!";
and in recognition of their providing a valuable
networking environment of pursuing wealth,
appreciating of fine cigars, maintaining limited public
involvement, and creating a safe, social outlet
for men and women of diverse, albeit dubious,
occupation and character.

Harvey L. Hall
Mayor of the City of Bakersfield

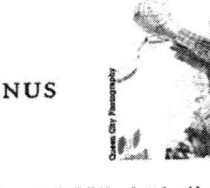

_he Cream of
THE CROP

	SCHOOL	RATIO
1	International Academy*—Bloomfield Hills, Mich.	6.323
2	Stanton College Prep*—Jacksonville, Fla.	5.639
3	Paxon*—Jacksonville, Fla.	4.668
4	Alabama School of Fine Arts—Birmingham, Ala.	4.567
5	Jericho—N.Y.	4.519
6	George Mason*—Falls Church, Va.	4.365
7	Myers Park*—Charlotte, N.C.	4.086
8	Science Academy of South Texas—Mercedes, Texas	4.024
9	H-B Woodlawn—Arlington, Va.	3.961
10	Los Angeles Center for Enriched Studies—Calif.	3.893
11	Manhasset—N.Y.	3.840
12	Wyoming—Cincinnati	3.782
13	Bellevue—Wash.	3.755
14	Highland Park—Dallas	3.693
15	Edgemont—Scarsdale, N.Y.	3.673
16	International—Bellevue, Wash.	3.643
17	Great Neck South—Great Neck, N.Y.	3.640
18	Newport—Bellevue, Wash.	3.625
19	Cold Spring Harbor—N.Y.	3.573
20	Mills University Studies—Little Rock, Ark.	3.564
21	Lincoln Park Academy*—Ft. Pierce, Fla.	3.521
22	W.T. Woodson*—Fairfax, Va.	3.448
23	Yorktown—Arlington, Va.	3.422
24	St. Petersburg*—Fla.	3.403
25	Brighton—Rochester, N.Y.	3.357
26	Great Neck North—Great Neck, N.Y.	3.298
27	Greeley—Chappaqua, N.Y.	3.240
28	Washington-Lee*—Arlington, Va.	3.192
29	Wheatley—Old Westbury, N.Y.	3.146
30	Langley—McLean, Va.	3.144
31	Indian Hill—Cincinnati	3.100
32	Ft. Myers*—Fla.	3.075

OLDEST LIVING ALUMNUS AWARD ESTABLISHED

William Hopple '24 places great store in common sense. When the state of Ohio allowed him to renew his driver's license at the age of ninety-six, he immediately sold his car. "I have no interest in driving a car in a state where guys like me are allowed to drive," he told his seventy-three-year-old son, Ed Hopple. Thinking like that has allowed Hopple at the age of one hundred to become Kenyon's oldest living alumnus.

Thanks to a generous donation from the Hopple family, Kenyon's oldest living alumnus will now be honored each year, receiving a plaque to mark the achievement. In addition, a permanent plaque will stay at the College with the names of all those who earn the distinction engraved on it.

The title was not officially acknowledged until Ed came across an issue of the *Bulletin* while visiting his father. It dawned on Ed that his dad probably held the position, and Ed called Russell Geiger, Kenyon's director of major gifts, with the idea of endowing an award to honor his father's achievement.

"We had never really thought too much about it," says Geiger. "But we looked into it,

and sure enough, Bill Hopple is the oldest living alumnus and has been for about three years." Ed Hopple told Geiger he thought it would be nice to officially acknowledge his father and those to follow. Geiger agreed.

Born before the Wright brothers' first flight at Kitty Hawk, North Carolina, Hopple has been frugal and modest all of his life, but always generous with charities, family, and friends. "It takes character to buy a Chevy when you can afford a Cadillac," says Hopple.

He learned to value saving and investment during the Great Depression. As he made his way up through the ranks to become chairman of the Stearns and Foster mattress company, Hopple invested in the stock market steadily. And as his hard work and investments paid off, Hopple contributed regularly to Kenyon and other nonprofit organizations. He believed giving back to the community simply made good sense and eschewed any fuss made about his good works.

Hopple currently resides in a two-bedroom apartment in an assisted-living facility near Cincinnati, Ohio. His first wife, Mary, died in 1954, and he recently lost his second wife, Janet, after forty-six years of marriage. ◉

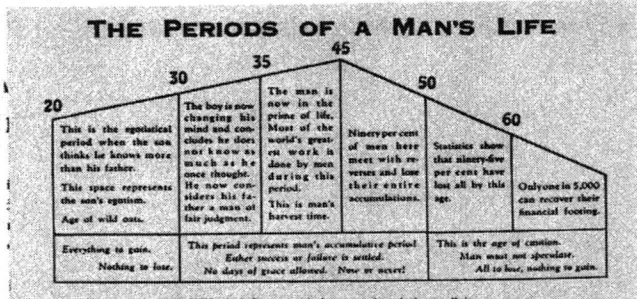

THE PERIODS OF A MAN'S LIFE

THIS TABLE IS FOR YOU   HOW DO YOU CHECK UP?

WHISKEY MADE AS OUR FATHERS MADE IT

JACK DANIEL DISTILLERY

LEM MOTLOW, PROPRIETOR

Placed in the National Register of Historic Places by the U.S. Government.

GOLD MEDALS AWARDED AT
ST. LOUIS, 1904
LIEGE, BELGIUM, 1905
GHENT, BELGIUM, 1913
ANGLO AMERICAN EXPORTION, LONDON, 1914
CERTIFICATE OF THE INSTITUTE
OF HYGIENE, LONDON, 1915
STAR OF EXCELLENCE, BRUSSELS, 1954
AMSTERDAM, 1981

WITNESSETH, that the said party or parties of the first part for and in consideration of the said party of the second part's avowed and generously expressed loyalty to and devotion for Jack Daniel's "Charcoal Mellowed" Whiskey and other valuable considerations rendered by the said party of the second part, the receipt of which is hereby acknowledged, does by these presents GRANT, CONVEY AND CONFIRM unto the said party of the second part the following title and rights of land pertaining to said title.

TENNESSEE SQUIRE

Deed

This deed made and entered into this day

Mar. 30, 1990

by the said owners and the below mentioned for the express purpose of conveying to:

Edwards R. Hopple

The following REAL ESTATE situated in the County of Moore and State of Tennessee, and more particularly described as Plot No. __61734__ as shown on an unrecorded plot, dated June 1, 1955, and being a part of the land conveyed unto the Jack Daniel Distillery, Lem Motlow, Proprietor, Inc., by Lem Motlow et al dated January 3rd, 1940, of record in Deed Book No. 20 Page 481 R. O. M. C., Tennessee, near The Hollow, the site still used for charcoal-mellowing Tennessee Whiskey drop by drop.

TO HAVE AND TO HOLD the same, together with all rights and appurtenances to the same belonging, unto the said party, and to the heirs and assigns of such party, forever

In Witness whereof the said party of the first part has here unto set their hand the day and year first above written.

JACK DANIEL DISTILLERY

BY _____

"GONE, BUT NEVER FORGOTTEN"

With this continuing commitment to the community it serves, Mercy is looking to the future. It is a future filled with new challenge and new promise. As the hospital plans for the next decade and beyond, there is an air of excitement and anticipation.

MERCY HOSPITAL
BOARD OF DIRECTORS

KERN COUNTY

1967 ROSTER

BAKERSFIELD CALIFORNIAN
P.O. BIN 440
323-7631

George P. DeArmond

July 30
Orland, Calif.
(MARY)

GEORGE

GREENFIELD STATE BANK
1530 TRUXTUN AVE.
323-6061

David Q. Vandermark

June 14
Los Angeles, Calif.
(LORABELLE)

DAVE

BAKERSFIELD ENGRAVING CO.
2201 So. UNION AVE.
831-0923

Victor Dallons

March 17
Kokoma, Ind.
(AGNES)

VIC

HILL HOUSE MOTEL
P.O. BOX 618
327-4064

Jeri Bruce

June 10
Ya'lville, Ark
(WARREN)

JERI

AD-VAN, INC.
400 TRUXTUN SUITE 103
324-4978

Kenneth Ramsey

Aug. 3
Kansas City, Mo.
(DOTTY)

KEN

BAKERSFIELD NATIONAL BANK
1300 22nd. STREET
324-8041

David E. Parker

June 20
Harrisburg, Ore.
(COLLEEN)

DAVE

BAKERSFIELD NEWS BULLETIN
P.O. BOX 236
327-7164

William A. Sanborn

May 3
Calgary Alberta
(BERTHA)

BILL

ADVERTISERS ADDRESSING SERVICE
1507 8th STREET
327-5191

William R. Anderson, Jr.

April 12
Wichita, Kansas
(FRANCES)

BILL

K. W. A. C. RADIO
5200 STANDARD STREET
327-9711

Edward R. Hopple

Jan. 6
Cincinnati, Ohio
(CATHARINE)

ED

K. B. A. K. TV
P. O. BOX 2929
327-7955

Simon D. Darrah

July 9
Millville, Calif.
(SHIRLEY)

SI

BAKERSFIELD CABLE TV
1516 V STREET
325-1271

Gary Hakenson

Sept. 28
National City, Calif.
(MARY)

GARY

BAZIUK AGENCY
354 HABERFELDE BLDG.
325-4359

Walter L. Baziuk

Oct. 26
Los Angeles, Calif.
(ISABELLE)

WALT

K. E. R. O. TV
P.O. BOX 2357
327-1441

Roderick E. O'Harra

April 27
Tama, Iowa
(LESLYN)

ROD

VALLEY PLAZA SHOPPING CENTER
MING AND WIBLE
832-2436

Reginald Jones

May 23
Winnipeg, Manitoba
(JUNE)

REG

BETTER BUSINESS BUREAU
1224 CHESTER AVE.
325-3823

Donald S. Hopkins

May 25
Whitefish, Mont.
(MILDRED)

DON

K. L. Y. D. RADIO
2831 EYE STREET
327-7511

Richard L. Venturino

Jan. 26
Oakland, Calif.
(SANDRA)

DICK

GOLDEN CRUST BAKERY
1512 M STREET
324-4014

Albert C. Robbins

Dec. 25
Harrison, N. J.
(LOUISE)

AL

K. E. R. N. RADIO
5600 FRASER RD.
832-1410

Edward E. Urner

Dec. 6
Bakersfield, Calif.
(GLORIA)

ED

K. U. Z. Z. RADIO
406 CHESTER AVE.
327-4401

Larry Daniels

July 22
Tulare, Calif.
(MARILYN)

LARRY

HUNTER PRINTING COMPANY
801 20th. STREET
325-6631

Walter E. Schuricht

April 22
Torrance, Calif.
(ALMA)

WALT

JEAN KITCHAK ART
413 CHESTER AVE.
324-1293

Jean A. Kitchak

Dec. 28
Taft, Calif.
(JOAN)

JEAN

KERN CABLE TV
P.O. BOX 1846
327-9671

John Calvetti

Feb. 16
Evanston, Illinois
(BEVERLY)

JOHN

OILDALE NEWS
P.O. BOX 5066
399-2375

Dorothy Hunsinger

June 29
Jonesboro, Ark.

DOTTY

PACIFIC GAS & ELECTRIC CO.
1918 "H" STREET
327-9561

William G. Rea, Jr.

Aug. 4
Bakersfield, Calif.
(LILLIAN)

BILL

SEARS ROEBUCK & COMPANY
3001 MING AVE.
832-2111

Howard H. Lackey

Dec. 29
Hartshorne, Okla.
(BEVERLY)

HOWARD

ALLENTHORP PHOTOGRAPHY
216 CHESTER AVE.
325-8621

Carl C. Allenthorp

Aug. 3
Delta, Colo.
(MARY)

CARL

BROCKS
1918 CHESTER AVE.
327-1731

Vernon O. Heitzenrader

April 20
Fresno, Calif.
(LUCILLE)

VERN

CALCOT LTD.
P.O. BOX 3217
327-5961

Vern Highley

July 18
Carterville, Mo.
(CARRIE)

VERN

CENTER NEON COMPANY
430 EAST 21st. STREET
324-8103

Wayne A. McNamer

Oct. 3
Bakersfield, Calif.
(GENEVA)

WAYNE

COAST SPECIALTIES
P.O. BOX 1386
323-4180

Frank DeShong

March 6
Arkadelphia, Ark.
(RUBY)

FRANK

FIRST AMERICAN TITLE CO.
1120 CALIFORNIA AVE.
327-5311

Robert Neal

July 24
Bakersfield, Calif.
(MARY)

BOB

K. L. Y. D. TV
2831 EYE STREET
327-7511

Emidio J. Battisti

Oct. 20
Elmira, New York
(LORRANE)

PAUL

LOVE & LEGGIO ADVERTISING
212 CHESTER AVE.
323-7589

Joseph Leggio

Dec. 6
South Gate, Calif.

JOE

MONTGOMERY WARD
3201 F STREET
327-4622

Stanley G. Tucker

May 17
New Haven, Conn.
(JUDITH)

STAN

K. B. I. S. RADIO
225 CHESTER AVE.
324.6093

Herbert H. Wisson

April 4
Rye, Colorado
(HELEN)

HERB

K. B. I. S. RADIO
225 CHESTER AVE.
324.6093

Ted Holmes

April 22
New York, N. Y.
(PEG)

TED

K. A. F. Y. RADIO
P.O. BOX 1448
366-4411

Mike Thomas

March 24
Cleveland, Ohio
(MAYLAND)

MIKE

Realtor®
(661) 836-6286 DIRECT
(661) 330-8737 CELL
(661) 836-0744 FAX
bmaheras@cbbakersfield.com

COLDWELL BANKER
PREFERRED REALTORS®
One University Centre
9100 Ming Ave., #100
Bakersfield, CA 93311

Each Office Is Independently Owned And Operated.

MICHAEL DUFFY
PHOTOGRAPHER

661-822-8374

E-mail: duffy@duffycom.com
P.O. Box 2177 Tehachapi, California 93581

M.A.R.E.
Mastering Abilities Riding Equines

Michelle Rasmussen
Executive Director

18240 Johnson Rd. • Bakersfield, CA 93312 • (661)589-1877 Fax (661)589-2310
www.bakersfield.org/mare • E-mail: mareridingcenter@aol.com

D2M Fly Fish

Custom Fly Rods & Fishing Toys

(970) 498-0884
Fax (970) 407-9516
d2miller@lamar.colostate.edu

DWAIN MILLER
1301 Buttonwood Drive
Fort Collins, CO 80525

CBIZ

Ann M. Braun
Director

CBIZ Accounting, Tax &
Advisory Services, LLC
5060 California Avenue, Suite 800
Bakersfield, CA 93309
Phone: 661.325.7500
Fax: 661.325.7004
abraun@cbiz.com

Offices in
Major Cities
Nationwide

Ben Janson
Retired Person

4525 Laclede Ave. #15
St. Louis, MO 63108

314-454-9435
FAX 314-454-9435
E-Mail BenJANSON@MSN.com

McCARTHY STEEL INC.
Steel Fabrication • Steel Sales
Industrial Supplies

Robert McCarthy
President

P.O. Box 89
313 South St.
San Luis Obispo, CA 93401
(805) 543-1760

P.O. Box 1887
3030 M St.
Bakersfield, CA 93303
(805) 324-6715

Fax (805) 324-6710

PHONE 324-9648

UNION *cemetery* ASSOCIATION
KING & POTOMAC
BAKERSFIELD, CALIFORNIA 93305

RUTHE N. WEST
SUPERINTENDENT

Box 3066
BAKERSFIELD, CA 93385

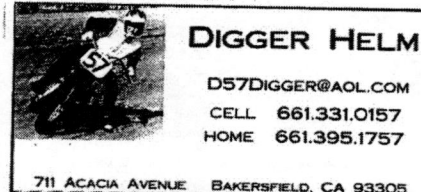
DIGGER HELM

D57DIGGER@AOL.COM

CELL 661.331.0157
HOME 661.395.1757

711 ACACIA AVENUE   BAKERSFIELD, CA 93305

22ND DISTRICT CALIFORNIA

KEVIN McCARTHY
MEMBER OF CONGRESS

1523 LONGWORTH BUILDING
WASHINGTON, DC 20515

202-225-2915
FAX: 202-225-2908

Escrow Administrator

1250 San Carlos Avenue, Suite 102
San Carlos, CA 94070
mtownson@InteroRealEstate.com
FAX 650.622.1099
CELL 650.766.9113
OFFICE 650.622.1000

DIRECT 650.622.1069

INTERO
REAL ESTATE SERVICES

FRANK J. CICONE LAW CORPORATION
5601 TRUXTUN AVENUE, SUITE 100
BAKERSFIELD, CALIFORNIA 93309

FRANK J. CICONE

(661) 327-2796
FAX (661) 327-3238

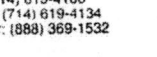

FROM KEN AND DOTTIE RAMSEY WITH THE 4-STAR FLAG FOR THE LIMO.

Official Flag of

General Rank

This is to certify that a General Rank
flag has been presented to

Edwards Hopple
(aka Major Hoople)

in recognition of his gallant services to mankind,
most notable of which was his leadership
in the Virgin Islands Campaign
and in particular the invasion of Jost Van Dyke
and getting shit-faced with "Foxy," himself.
It is to be duly noted that subsequent to this heroic action,
the Virgin Islands were renamed. It is most appropriate
that this distinguished award is presented in conjunction
with that glorious holiday of holidays,
St. Paddy's Day.
Executed on March 17, 2004.

Wes Point
Wes Point, Secretary of the Army

Laurel N. Hardy
Laurel N. Hardy, Secretary of Defense

Ron Purdy
Ron Purdy, Songleader

David Vordermark
David Vordermark, Historian, Virgin Islands

Monica Lewinski
Monica Lewinski, Under the Secretary of the Army

W.C. Feels
W.C. Feels, Secretary of Offense

Ralph Nater
Ralph Nater, Concierge

Betsie Ross
Betsie Ross, Flag Booking Agent

HOW LONG DO WE HAVE?

This is a democracy countdown . . . you may have heard of it.

About the time the original thirteen states adopted their new constitution in 1787, Alexander Tyler, a Scottish history professor at the University of Edinburgh, had this to say about the fall of the Athenian Republic some 2,000 years earlier:

"A democracy is always temporary in nature; it simply cannot exist as a permanent form of government."

"A democracy will continue to exist up until the time that voters discover they can vote themselves generous gifts from the public treasury."

"From that moment on, the majority always vote for the candidates who promise the most benefits from the public treasury, with the result that every democracy will finally collapse due to loose fiscal policy, which is always followed by a dictatorship."

"The average age of the world's greatest civilizations from the beginning of history, has been about 200 years."

"During those 200 years, those nations always progressed through the following sequence:

1. From bondage to spiritual faith;
2. From spiritual faith to great courage;
3. From courage to liberty;
4. From liberty to abundance;
5. From abundance to complacency;
6. From complacency to apathy;
7. From apathy to dependence;
8. From dependence back into bondage.

Professor Joseph Olson of Hemline University School of Law, St. Paul, Minnesota, points out some interesting facts concerning the 2000 Presidential election"

Number of state won by: Democrats = 19; Republicans—29

Square Miles of Land won by: Democrats = 580,000; Republicans—2,427,000

Population of counties (in millions) won by: Democrats = 127; Republicans—143

Murder rate per 100,000 residents in counties won by Democrats = 13.2; Republican = 2.1

Professor Olsen adds: "In aggregate, the map of the territory Republicans won was mostly the land owned by the taxpaying citizens of this great country. Democratic territory mostly encompassed those citizens living in government owned tenements and living off various forms of government welfare. He believes the US is now somewhere between "complacency and apathy" . . . with some forty percent of the nation's population having reached the "governmental dependency" phase.

If congress grants amnesty and citizenship to twenty million criminal invaders called illegal's, and they vote, then we can say goodbye to the USA in fewer than five years.

Thanks to Bebe Burke for sending me this.

HOME

The Christmas House On Elm Street

What does "Rubik's Cube", "PacMan" or the "Olympics" have to do with Christmas? Or for that matter, with our "home" feature? Read on and you'll learn that what started out as a "bet" has become a tradition at the Ed and Cathie Hopple home on Elm Street.

This stately home, encompassing two large lots, was originally built in 1940 and was acquired by the Hopples in 1969. As one might imagine of a home from that era, it is graced with classic architectural design, exquisite crown moldings, and a sweeping staircase that highlights a most impressive entry hall.

But despite all of the home's distinctive features, it's the personality and creativeness of it's owners that distinguishes it as one of Bakersfield's most popular residences.

For the past nine years, ever since a friend bet Ed that he couldn't decorate the huge pine tree that graces their front yard, the Hopples have created spectacular Christmas fantasies for all to admire. Giant Rubik's Cubes, a PacMan, an Olympic skier coming down the roof, a larger-than-life Cabbage Patch doll, and other themes have brought delight to young and old each holiday season. Add to the theme thousands of brightly colored lights adorning the exterior of the home and huge trees, and nothing short of Disneyland could compare. Ed says "I'm the only guy in Bakersfield with 125 extension cords."

Both Ed and Cathie give credit to family and friends for creating the spectacular decorations each year. About the first of November they start collecting ideas and then hold one giant decorating party when the entire outside of their home comes alive with the spirit of the season.

Ed, who is the owner/manager of KWAC radio, is well known in the community for his civic involvement. Cathie has been a member of the Mercy Hospital Auxiliary for more than 22 years, working the admitting desk and supervising 70 members of the Junior Auxiliary Candy Stripers.

Even though they both lead hectic work schedules, they always find time for family, friends and the home where mail arrives simply addressed to *"The Christmas House on Elm Street."*

Get Published, Inc!
Thorofare, NJ 08086
16 October 2009
BA2009289